MICHAŁ KALECKI ON A SOCIALIST ECONOMY

Also by Jerzy Osiatyński

CAPITAL, DISTRIBUTION AND VALUE (*in Polish*)
KALECKI'S COLLECTED WORKS (*editor, in Polish*)

Michał Kalecki on a Socialist Economy

Jerzy Osiatyński

Translated by Jan Toporowski

St. Martin's Press New York

First published in the United States of America in 1988

Printed in Hong Kong

ISBN 0–312–01562–3

Library of Congress Cataloging-in-Publication Data
Osiatyński, Jerzy.
Michał Kalecki on a socialist economy/Jerzy Osiatyński;
translated by Jan Toporowski.
p. cm.
Translated from Polish.
Bibliography: p.
Includes index.
ISBN 0–312–01562–3 : $47.50 (est).
1. Poland—Economic policy—1945 —2. Kalecki, Michał. I. Title.
HC340.3.085 1988
338.9438—dc19 87–33093
CIP

Contents

Preface

This book arose out of my research on the work of Michał Kalecki on the theory and practice of the socialist economy. This research was undertaken in preparing the third and fourth volumes of Kalecki's *Collected Works*,[1] comprising his work on this subject. The papers that I discovered in the archives of the Council of Ministers and the Planning Commission confirm the unusually close link between Kalecki's theories and his activity as an expert and adviser to the highest economic authorities. In so far as it is possible, I would like to make available to the reader an account of this aspect of Kalecki's work, which is today unknown and partly forgotten, and its influence on his theoretical ideas. This will also enable certain important themes in the recent history of Polish economic thought and in post-war Polish economic history to be brought out of obscurity. This is the first aim of my book.

Kalecki did not leave behind any work which systematically deals with the whole range of problems of socialist reproduction, a work which could be the counterpart to his *Theory of Economic Dynamics* of the capitalist economy.[2] He himself never tried to bring together his reflections on various aspects of the socialist economy. My second purpose in writing this book has been to try to bring together the various fragments and elements of Kalecki's theory and, on this basis, to reconstruct his views on the functioning and development of a socialist economy.

At the same time, I have tried to present not only the directions in which Kalecki's ideas evolved, but also the criticisms with which they met, and the course of further theoretical researches by other economists, as well as the issues that remain unresolved.

The career of the central character of this book, and the close connection between his theoretical work and economic practice in Poland have determined the manner of presenting his contribution to this branch of knowledge. This book has a narrative-analytical character. This allows the theoretical work of Kalecki to be placed in its actual socio-economic context, and to be applied to the real process of Polish economic development. The narrative theme therefore provides a natural background to the analysis. Nevertheless, I have tried to ensure that the former does not predominate over the latter, or precipitate the loss of the necessary distance that is required in assessing the work of Kalecki.

In the course of my research on Kalecki's work, many colleagues and friends have helped and advised me, and many have encouraged me to write this book. I am deeply grateful for this help, advice and encouragement. I would also like to thank my Polish publishers, Państwowe Wydawnictwo Ekonomiczne, who have allowed me to make extensive use in this book of the notes and commentaries in the third and fourth volumes of Kalecki's *Collected Works*.

JERZY OSIATYŃSKI

Notes

1. M. Kalecki, *Dzieła* (*Collected Works*), Państwowe Wydawnictwo Ekonomiczne (PWE), Warsaw, vol. III (1982), vol. IV (1984)
2. M. Kalecki, *Theory of Economic Dynamics* (London: George Allen & Unwin, 1954).

Foreword

Michał Kalecki (1899–1970) belongs to the few Polish economists who left an indelible mark on the development of economic thought worldwide. His reputation in the West rests however mainly on his seminal contribution to the theory of dynamics of the capitalist economy, where – to quote Lawrence Klein – 'Kalecki's greatest achievement, among many, was undoubtedly his complete anticipation of Keynes' *General Theory*'.[1] His work on socialist economy is much less known outside Poland, and perhaps several other socialist countries.

In English, apart from a small number of papers dispersed among not always easily accessible journals, the main sample of Kalecki's own writings on socialism is his *Introduction to the Theory of Growth in a Socialist Economy* included also in the volume of *Selected Essays on the Economic Growth of the Socialist and the Mixed Economy* brought together by Kalecki himself shortly before his death.[2] His work on other issues of socialist economics, particularly those related to the system of functioning (economic mechanism) has been made known to the English reader only in part and indirectly through the intermediary of books devoted to Kalecki and his economics in general, such as G. R. Feiwel's *The Intellectual Capital of Michał Kalecki* or M. C. Sawyer's *The Economics of Michał Kalecki*; among the rather rare articles on the subject of socialist economics D. M. Nuti's 'Michał Kalecki's Contribution to the Theory and Practice of Socialist Planning' stands out recently.[3]

Jerzy Osiatyński's book is much more than an addition to this slim list, and not only because it is devoted entirely to Kalecki's economics of socialism. The singularity of this book lies in the fact that it is based on meticulous research of both Kalecki's published work and of the mass of the hitherto unpublished archival material: records of meetings in which Kalecki participated (including discussions in the advisory Economic Council of Poland in the late 1950s), his correspondence, memos written in his capacity as adviser to central planning authorities and head of the Polish delegation to the Economic Commission of the Council of Mutual Economic Assistance (Comecon). The wealth of material of this type not merely makes one aware of the close links between Kalecki's theoretical work and his activity in planning practice, which is rightly stressed by the author in his own Preface, but also puts every piece of Kalecki's writings into a proper context, allowing the reader to judge the argument against the background of an adequate presentation of the issues in question and of other views on the matter. Although the book should by no means be seen as a simple compilation of Kalecki's writings enriched by the related archival material – this is Osiatyński's own book with original analysis leading to a valiant attempt at a synthesis in the concluding chapter – one is justified in treating much of the contents as an authentic, first-hand source. The author himself intends apparently to convey this idea by choosing the title *Michał Kalecki on a Socialist Economy*, which is both modest and accurate. As I have had the privilege to work closely with Kalecki on a number of theoretical and practical problems of a socialist economy, I can appreciate this in full.

Invited to write this foreword, I first contemplated writing a brief essay. However, having studied the book carefully, I finally decided against this because it became clear to me that there was very little which could be added to the text itself by way of useful introduction. The picture of Kalecki's economics of socialism – both his methodological approach and his substantive conclusions – emerges from Osiatyński's book clearly and comprehensively. Needless to say, much of it is controversial and subject to various interpretations, but all is in my view highly relevant not only to the problems of the 'really existing' (that is, the communist version of) socialism, but to any kind of socialist alternative.

WŁODZIMIERZ BRUS

Notes

1. Lawrence R. Klein, foreword to *The Intellectual Capital of Michał Kalecki. A Study in Economic Theory and Policy*, by G. R. Feiwel (Knoxville: University of Tennessee Press, 1975).
2. Michał Kalecki, *Introduction to the Theory of Growth in a Socialist Economy* Oxford: Basil Blackwell, 1969); *Selected Essays on the Economic Growth of the Socialist and the Mixed Economy* (Cambridge University Press, 1972).
3. G. R. Feiwel, see n. 1 above; M. C. Sawyer, *The Economics of Michał Kalecki* (London and Basingstoke: Macmillan, 1985); D. M. Nuti, 'Michał Kalecki's Contribution to the Theory and Practice of Socialist Planning', *Cambridge Journal of Economics*, vol. x, no. 4 (December 1986), pp 333–53.

1 The Democratically Planned Economy

LINKS WITH THE INTELLECTUAL LEFT IN THE 1930s

Michał Kalecki's first economic articles were concerned with studies of various commodity markets, and the structure and activities of major Polish and foreign firms in inter-war Poland. These studies became the basis of more theoretical analyses which he published in, among others, *Przegląd Socjalistyczny* (*Socialist Review*). Kalecki was actively involved with this journal from its establishment in December 1931 right up to the time of its suspension by the police in 1932.

Przegląd Socjalistyczny was a radical paper that was addressed primarily to left-wing intellectuals. It was not an organ of the Polish Communist Party. Rather, its programme was modelled on that of the British Independent Labour Party. The editor was a philosopher and economist, Antoni Pański, a pupil of a Polish philosopher of worldwide reputation, Tadeusz Kotarbiński.[1] The journal's character was well reflected in the editorial programme that appeared in its first edition. This announced that:

> Whenever the present crisis ends, and whatever may be its *dénouement*, this cruel lesson on the nature of capitalism which the crisis has inflicted on humanity must bear its fruit . . . We are witnessing the moral suicide of this system. However long that system may continue to vegetate, human thought will turn with increasing resolution and impatience to an order in which society will regulate its economy in a *planned* way, and in which today's decisive motive force, capitalist profits, is excluded; in other words to *socialism* . . .
>
> . . . We regard our task to be to provide a critical analysis of the most important aspects of social and economic activity, to follow the development of the socialist movement in all its manifestations, to elucidate the problems facing it, and to record the stages leading up to the establishment of socialism wherever it may be being

> advanced. We seek to express, in so far as we are able, all that is of interest to the socialist movement, and that in which the socialist movement must interest itself.[2]

The programme contained in this declaration was developed and in certain respects made more specific in Kalecki's article that came immediately after it, entitled 'The World Financial Crisis'.[3]

According to the recollection of persons who knew Kalecki in the 1920s, from at least the time when his studies at the Gdańsk Polytechnic were broken off in 1925, he had decidedly radical views and was associated with left-wing movements. In the following years, and especially with the prolonged economic crisis of 1929–33, Kalecki's convictions and activities underwent a further radicalisation, similar in fact to those of Oskar Lange and the group associated with the journal *Płomienie* (*Flames*), and organised in the Związek Niezaleznej Młodzieży Socjalistycznej (the Union of Independent Socialist Youth).[4]

Another factor influencing the character of the articles published by Kalecki in these years was the development of National Socialism in Germany. In many of his articles he warned against the danger of this phenomenon.

CONTACTS WITH THE BRITISH LABOUR PARTY

The earnestness of Kalecki's criticism of capitalism in his early articles leaves no doubt that he was committed to the cause of socialism. However, at that time the theoretical problems of the socialist economy did not yet engage his attention. In England, from 1936, he continued his research on the theory of the business cycle. He also worked on the question of the distribution of income under oligopolistic capitalism and the statistical verification of his theoretical hypotheses. From the outbreak of the Second World War he almost wholly occupied himself with the problems of the British war economy. It was only in Oxford that he established closer contacts with active members of the Labour Party, which already in the 1930s had placed the notion of a planned economy at the head of its programme. This prompted Kalecki to shift his attention from the current problems of the war economy to the problems of how a socialist economy might operate.

In the autumn of 1942, at the invitation of the Socialist Clarity

Group, a discussion group operating on the fringes of the Labour Party whose membership included Labour Party activists and non-members, Kalecki delivered a lecture under the title 'The Minimum Essentials of Democratic Planning'.[5] Despite the general character of this statement, it contained a very realistic appraisal of the political preconditions for socialist planning. He considered that the primary precondition for the introduction of economic planning was the break-up of the class power of the major capitalist groups:

> As long as the influence of monopoly capitalists over society as a whole exists, all the efforts of the workers in the factories and through the Trade Unions to diminish this direct power of the capitalists over the workers can only have limited success. The fight for workers' rights in industry and for more effective workers' representation, through such things as Works' Councils and Production Committees, is, of course, of very great importance and . . . has a vital part to play in the *total* struggle against the capitalists. But it can never be a *substitute* for the necessary political fight to destroy the power wielded over society as a whole by the great capitalist interest-groups.[6]

Kalecki considered that the establishment of state control over the system of banking and finance, investment and foreign trade and so on, through the full nationalisation of these 'commanding heights' of the economy, or through the creation among them of some form of state enterprises, was insufficient to break the economic, political and social power of monopoly capital. Besides, he saw the very establishment of such control as being dependent on mass social support. This in turn would only arise from a widespread conviction that such a policy would guarantee rapid economic development and, in consequence, full employment and steady improvements in the material condition of society. But gaining broad mass support alone did not appear to him to be a sufficient condition for overcoming the power of large capital. To achieve this it was necessary, in Kalecki's opinion, to introduce direct social control. The creation of its organisational and institutional forms and foundations he counted among the first steps that should be taken by a socialist government.[7]

The effect of a socialist government's policy 'from above', and social pressure 'from below', was seen by Kalecki as a cumulative process of social revolution, without which democratic socialist planning would remain a chimera. For this reason, he warned a future socialist government not to fear the economic consequences of a developing process of social revolution, and cautioned it against suppressing the enthusiasm of the workers, as did the Popular Front Government in France, for example. Instead, this enthusiasm should be used against the enemies of democratic planning.

In this statement, Kalecki also drew attention to two questions of fundamental importance for the theory of the socialist economy. The first was the institutional structure of socialist planning and its essential dissimilarity to planning in a capitalist enterprise, or planning as an element of state interventionism. (Kalecki returned to this theme many times in his subsequent work on the theory of growth of a socialist economy, and the theory of capitalist economic dynamics.) The second question was the relationship between the autonomy of workers' direct control, and the domain of central planning and central economic control. He returned to these problems after more than a decade in completely different institutional and political circumstances in his essay *Workers' Councils and Central Planning*.[8]

PROBLEMS OF POST-WAR RECONSTRUCTION

From March 1945 Kalecki worked for the International Labour Office in Montreal, where he was occupied with the problems of post-war economic reconstruction. At the end of 1945 he was invited back to Poland by the Ministry of Reconstruction, to give expert advice on the economic situation of the country, and the best methods of organising its reconstruction.

> The greatest problem that we are grappling with at present [wrote the Minister of Reconstruction, Michał Kaczorowski, in his letter of invitation] is the adaptation of our financial and monetary policy to our existing productive possibilities and, linked to this problem, the establishment of an appropriate programme of reconstruction. For this reason, your opinion on the possibilities of co-ordinating our material and human resources with our monetary policy would be unusually welcome in this country.[9]

In August 1946, Kalecki arrived in Warsaw. In the course of a three-month stay he prepared his *Observations on Rationing and the Price System*, with some supplementary notes, *Observations on Savings and Money Circulation in Poland*, and *Financial Plans for the Second Half of 1946 and the First Half of 1947.*[10]

The organisation of markets and prices in the initial period after the liberation of Poland from German occupation was based on differentiated prices in two sets of markets: controlled and free. In the controlled markets, the prices of essential raw materials, industrial and agricultural goods and basic consumer articles, together with wages, interest rates, tax rates and the prices of public services were fixed. In the free markets, prices equilibrating supply and demand prevailed. The intervention of the state in these markets was aimed at expanding supplies where possible. The traditional instruments of financial policy were used. Corresponding to this differentiation of markets was a differentiation among consumers according to their access to regulated markets.

In the agricultural year 1944–45, the food supply campaign was completed almost without any central budget subsidies. The prices paid to farmers for compulsory deliveries were fixed at the level of the prices in the regulated markets, so that the cost of the operation fell on the farmers. Additional sources of supply were deliveries from the United Nations Relief and Rehabilitation Administration (UNRRA). In the second half of 1945, and in 1946, around four-fifths of Polish imports came from this source. UNRRA aid was aimed at relieving the most urgent needs of the population for food, shoes and clothing, sanitary and medical equipment, as well as assisting in rebuilding and organising production and distribution. In the first half of 1947, UNRRA aid fell to 45 per cent, and in the second half to 21 per cent of the value of total imports, despite the fact that, in 1947, commercial imports had not yet reached their level of 1938.

In 1944–5, neither of these sources of supplies for regulated markets required significant financial resources from the government, which only had to finance the costs of administering purchases, storage, and eventual processing. The situation changed radically in the agricultural year of 1945–6, due mainly to the following factors.

The first was the unrealistically high quotas set for compulsory deliveries, sometimes exceeding not only the farmer's marketable surplus, but also his net output. The burden on agriculture, if these deliveries had been made at the compulsory purchase price, would have amounted to around 42 billion złoty in 1945–6, an amount which considerably exceeded the real possibilities of the rural sector.[11]

Secondly, whilst immediately after the war farmers, with few exceptions, discharged their obligations in respect of agricultural levies relatively well, in areas of military operations, as well as in previously liberated areas, the regularity of deliveries fell away as these operations shifted westwards. This was aggravated by the low prices (strictly tied to the prices paid by consumers in regulated markets) paid to farmers for their compulsory deliveries, relative to the prices of industrial articles purchased by them.

The purely economic consequences of these factors were as follows:

(1) failure to deliver quotas that were set at unrealistically high levels;
(2) the necessity to pay bonuses and other supplementary payments for punctual deliveries of the supplies that farmers possessed;
(3) the need to supplement inadequate compulsory deliveries with imported supplies or purchases on the free market;
(4) the low, practically unchanged, level of consumer prices in the regulated markets, and rising costs of agricultural and food procurement gave rise to a large budget deficit which had to be eliminated if the hitherto existing system of food supply was to continue in operation.

In mid-1946, faced with growing difficulties in enforcing compulsory deliveries, the Council of Ministers decided to abolish them with effect from 1 August. A major consideration behind this decision, in addition to those described above, was the political situation, with a major constitutional referendum and the first post-war general election approaching. From 1 August, food supplies in urban areas were to be secured by purchases on the free market at free market prices. The abolition of compulsory deliveries was accompanied by an announcement by the Minister for Industry, Hilary Minc, that in the agricultural year 1946–7 industry would supply the rural sector with commodities valued at nearly 1 billion pre-war złoty, or 50 billion post-war złotys. It was the linking up of this operation with the purchase of agricultural output that was to form the basis of the new system of exchange between the rural and the urban sectors.

Tied up with the elimination of compulsory deliveries was the problem of reforming the system of rationing. Instead of the various categories and entitlements in kind then in operation, a uniform scheme of rationing was proposed for the non-agricultural population, excluding traders, industrialists and persons with high private incomes. The eventual total abolition of rationing and monetary compensation for its present beneficiaries was also suggested. Taking into account all aspects of this situation, and using his experiences of wartime rationing in Britain, of which he had been a notable critic and proponent, Kalecki prepared his *Observations on Rationing and the Price System*, for the use of the Central Planning Office (*Centralny Urząd Planowania*) and for Hilary Minc. In this analysis, he concentrated above all on three issues:

(1) the advisability of continuing to ration basic articles of consumption;
(2) price differentiation for industrial products; and
(3) trading margins.

Since rationing involves subsidising the prices of essential articles of consumption for certain groups of consumers, in examining the arguments for and against rationing, Kalecki drew attention to two matters. First of all, in his view, rationing has the advantage that it secures for the consumer a constant real value of consumption. In view of this, the monetary compensation which consumers would receive after the lifting of rationing should have a fixed real value in proportion to the size of the ration and the difference between the free market price and the ration price, and it should also rise in the same proportion as any increase in the free market prices of hitherto rationed articles. Kalecki considered this to be the first condition for abolishing rationing.

Secondly, the trader's margin is significantly greater in the case of free market prices than in the case of administered prices. Thus, it is only possible to give up rationing when the loss to the consumer, due to higher trading margins, is more than compensated for by other benefits. Kalecki recommended the lifting of rationing of, for instance, bread and potatoes, since the savings in administrative costs together with wastage in distribution would undoubtedly be greater than the losses to the consumer from a higher trader's margin. He considered that it was also possible to give up rationing clothing: the clothing available on rations was often of low quality, but listed as standard quality, thereby allowing large-scale corruption to occur. But he considered it useful to retain the rationing of sugar, preserves, fats, cheeses, milk, cigarettes and other items.

Kalecki considered that the retail prices of non-rationed industrial articles were excessively differentiated, which was detrimental since this facilitated abuse. Even if establishing a uniform system of prices (by increasing the prices of industrial goods produced in the state sector) were to lead, for instance, to an increase in the costs of uniforms for the army, or higher building costs for the Ministry of Construction, the revenue of the clothing or construction industries would rise by exactly the same amount without upsetting overall financial equilibrium.

The standardisation of retail prices for the goods produced in the state sector was linked with a reduction in the trader's margins. Kalecki considered them to be an important cause of disproportionately higher incomes in the free market sector compared to those in the state sector. In order to prevent retailers from passing on the increase in supply prices, resulting from price standardisation, decisive intervention was necessary on the part of the state retail network, and regular checks on traders' margins by the state administration.

In his *Observations on Savings and Money Circulation in Poland* written for the Ministry of Finance, Kalecki presented the factors delimiting the issue of money. The increase in the demand for money in post-war Poland was, in Kalecki's opinion, primarily by the increase in the money circulating among enterprises and the population. This in turn was due to the rise in turnover resulting from price increases and the growth of production and supply. Taking these factors into account it was possible to estimate the stable, or at least only moderately inflationary, boundaries to the possible increases in the emission of money to finance the expenses of the state sector. He dealt with this question directly in *Financial Plans*.

The basis of the *Financial Plans for the Second Half of 1946 and the First Half of 1947* was an analysis of the supply and demand for money, which Kalecki based on a general plan of financial flows in the economy, the first to be drawn up in post-war Poland. The essence of both plans was a comparison of the financial requirements of the state sector with the funds available to meet them from savings, in the broad sense. In this category he included the profits of state trade and industry, insurance and special funds, assistance from UNRRA and other sources, and the capacity of markets to absorb money. The individual branches of the public sector had their net requirements entered into the Financial Plan as a deficit or surplus. The increase in the issue of money that was over and above that which could be absorbed by markets without inflationary pressure on prices, appeared in the Plan as the difference between the net financial requirement of the public sector, and the availability of funds, other than additional money issue, to meet them. Where possible the monetary surplus was to be eliminated by appropriate changes in the plan.

The significance of the financial plans proposed by Kalecki was enormous. Establishing planning as the foundation for economic organisation was one of the fundamental points of the government's programme after Liberation. But the first piecemeal plans worked out and implemented in 1946 – the Resolution of the National People's Council (*Krajowa Rada Narodowa*) of 21 September 1946, which laid down the principles of economic management based on national economic planning, and the law establishing the Three Year Plan for Economic Reconstruction – all had one important shortcoming: none of them had a distinct financial plan. A financial plan was not even prepared for the Economic Reconstruction Plan for 1947, which was part of the Three Year Plan, and although the Ministry of Finance was supposed to draw up a financial plan for 1948, this was not done. Similarly, the Plan for 1949 did not contain a financial plan: it was decided then that this should be worked out with a three-month delay.

There were many reasons for this situation. Of decisive significance were ideological and political considerations, and the ensuing change in the system of economic planning, from monetary control and planning by financial aggregates, advocated by the Central Planning Office and the Polish Socialist Party, towards physical planning and administrative distribution, supported by the Polish Workers' Party (Polska Partia Robotnicza – PPR) and Hilary Minc in particular. As the position of the Central Planning Office weakened, so the economy became increasingly a quasi-money economy, in which the planning of financial flows was limited to the balance of the population's incomes and expenditure, reflecting merely the overall equilibrium in consumer markets. In 1949, the once socialist-controlled Central Planning Office was replaced by the Communist-controlled State Commission for Economic Planning (*Państwowa Komisja Planowania Gospodarczego*).

In these circumstances, attempts to organise a Department of Finance in the Central Planning Office proved inconclusive, and attempts to incorporate all financial planning in the Finance Ministry encountered similar difficulties. In effect, the Three Year Plan and annual Reconstruction Plans only dealt with the distribution of physical commodities, in natural units aggregated at notional prices, without a financial counterpart to it. Because of this, the problem of inflationary pressures was also not adequately dealt with in these plans.

The absence of a financial policy was only partially filled by the preparation on time of government budgets and credit plans for the banking system. Kalecki's endeavour to construct a financial plan for the economy as a whole, and his explanation of the principles governing its preparation, created the possibility of filling this gap as early as the start of 1947, if the political climate had only been favourable. But though his plans probably were considered by the Polish National Bank (the Polish central bank), they were not implemented. His scheme for constructing financial plans was also not used, except as background material to work on the budget.

During his stay in Poland in the summer of 1946, Kalecki considered the possibility of a permanent return to Poland soon after. But he knew that to secure himself the position of an effective adviser, he needed to make favourable contacts with institutions and persons who were influential in the government, and above all, with Hilary Minc, who had already established himself under the Lublin Government in 1944 as the decisive voice in economic policy-making, and who also had what was for those times an unusually efficient executive apparatus at his disposal, which obeyed his instructions to the letter.

Kalecki's efforts to establish such links were not, however, effective at this time. This was presumably because of the distrust in which leading members of the Polish Workers' Party held him. In these circles, Kalecki's authority as an economist was respected, but he was regarded as an 'incomplete Marxist', which inevitably made acceptance of his ideas more difficult. This combination of respect and distrust led to a fear of the consequences of establishing him more permanently in some Government agency or department.

It appears that the 'incomplete Marxism' which was held against Kalecki at that time was not, in the interpretation of the communist Polish Workers' Party (PPR) leadership, based on an insufficiently 'class approach' on his part to economic matters. In these matters, Kalecki's attitude was quite close to that of the Party. He wholeheartedly disliked the bourgeoisie and capitalism. He was convinced of the need to reduce the share of capitalists' profits in national income, and he was very sensitive to the problem of unemployment. Like many PPR activists he did not attach much significance to the so-called 'model solutions' that were then espoused by some economists as an answer to the problem of planning in a mixed economy, although his views in this respect were to change in the 1960s. The fundamental difference consisted in his decided opposition to '*blitzkrieg*' tactics in achieving economic objectives. He never regarded the economy as a 'battle front', he opposed the use of unrealistic 'mobilising' plan indicators, and so on. This attitude was in distinct contrast to the approach of Hilary Minc and his entourage.

According to those who knew Kalecki at this time, he rapidly became aware of this difference in approach, and the direction in which the political situation was evolving in Poland. This was what chiefly predisposed him to return to Montreal. The recollection of his wife and his close friends and associates is that the growing wave of anti-semitism, which was expressed *inter alia* in the pogrom of Jews in Kielce on 4 July 1944 and its aftermath, also had a strong influence on Kalecki's eventual decision to leave Poland.

RATIONALISING THE POLISH ECONOMY, 1955–56

From the end of 1946 to the end of 1954, Kalecki worked as an assistant director in the Economic Department of the United Nations Secretariat in New York. After his return to Warsaw, at the end of February 1955, he took up the post of adviser to Hilary Minc, who was then the First Deputy Prime Minister. This was the final period of Minc's political and economic ascendancy. Partly because of illness, he needed the assistance of a competent and independently-minded adviser and this time he attached great hopes to his work with Kalecki, often emphasising later that he had learnt much from him. As adviser to Minc, his formal sphere of activity was very broad, taking in annual and longer-term plans, the general dimensions of those plans, income distribution, consumption and investment. He also advised on prices, foreign trade and the balance of payments. In practice, however, he dealt with matters of secondary importance.[12]

Kalecki's return to Poland coincided with a period of especially intense discussions inside the party leadership on these very issues of the general proportions of production, distribution and so on. These discussions took place in and around the Third Plenum of the Central Committee of the Polish United Workers' Party. Kalecki, who was not a Party member, did not take part in these disputes, partly because he did not wish to range himself on the side of any party faction, but mainly because of the closed, intra-party character of the debate. Most of 1955 he spent studying the problems of post-war growth in the developed capitalist countries. Only as the political situation clarified itself at the end of that year did he involve himself in the work of a special commission that was set up to review the financial system of state enterprises, and the work being conducted by the Planning Commission on changes in the methodology of economic planning.

In his early contributions to these two areas of discussion Kalecki emphasised the *gradual* process of rationalising the Polish economy. His attitude towards this question is well represented by two statements, in December 1955 and in the following January. In a memorandum to Minc entitled *The Decentralisation of Management in Small Industrial Businesses*, he started with three observations.[13] First of all, there were serious difficulties attendant upon applying the principle of central economic planning to small businesses with a diverse and constantly changing product mix. Such planning in such circumstances required a very large administrative apparatus. Secondly, controlling the prices of articles produced by co-operatives was very arduous, and the differences between these prices and those of similar articles produced by state enterprises gave scope for corruption and abuse. Thirdly, the present system of management did not provide adequate incentives for the proper utilisation of waste materials by small industrial businesses.

In this situation, Kalecki proposed that small state and co-operative enterprises in industry should be at least partially excluded from the scope of economic planning, and have their activities based on the principles of free market operations, or on long-term contracts with the public sector. At the same time, he opposed the proposal to base economic planning on a mechanistic system of 'automatic incentives'. He considered that this would in practice either lead to chaos, or else would require such complex adjustments that the economic administration system would become even more complicated.

He took a similar view during a conference organised at the end of January 1956 to discuss the problems of material incentives under socialism. He considered that even the best of incentives could not bring about an 'economic miracle' in the sense that they could not remove the actual obstacles to rising living standards. He regarded these obstacles as being exogenous, arising out of the insufficient growth of domestic agricultural production, and difficulties in balancing foreign trade. The introduction of a new system of incentives would not, in his opinion, resolve these difficulties, either directly or in the short term. However, despite this, it was worthwhile continuing to work on establishing the right system of incentives, since . . . 'it is precisely when serious difficulties of an objective nature are met that every contribution, however partial, towards overcoming them is important'.[14]

Kalecki saw two possible approaches to resolving the problem of incentives. The first depended on applying methods which would be easy to introduce in practice. Even if they did not remove all the shortcomings of the current structure of incentives, such steps could at least improve it significantly. The second would, in essence, change and reconstruct the whole incentives system.

Kalecki saw the preconditions for the gradual removal of weaknesses in the incentives system as being:

1. the relative stabilisation of salaries of technical personnel and management in enterprises, through a reduction in the contribution of bonuses to their overall earnings, and a relative increase in basic salaries;
2. the introduction of variable bonuses, related to the degree of fulfilment of the production plan, starting with a bonus at, say, 85 per cent plan fulfilment, which bonus would then increase by degrees up to, say, 115 per cent plan fulfilment;
3. making bonus payments dependent not on the fulfilment of a plan for the value of total output, but on the carrying out of a net output plan: that is, planned total production, calculated in constant prices *after* deducting the cost of materials and bought-in semi-finished goods. This was aimed at limiting the tendency to shift production to materials-intensive output, as a way of increasing the value of *total* output;
4. calculating the value of enterprise production not at supply prices, but according to factory gate prices, worked out by adding to materials and labour costs the same percentage margin to cover overheads and profits for all items of production;
5. a move away from raising the work quotas of employees on piece-work in line with rising labour productivity, eliminating the tendency for the actual level of pay per unit of outpout to be reduced in proportion to the increase in the productivity of the worker: the effect of this was a tendency to limit the growth of labour productivity.

These relatively small improvements could not, however, remove the incentive that the enterprise would still have to try to reduce the production plan handed down to it, or to seek to carry out quantitative production tasks at the cost of quality. Moreover, like all formulae used for calculating costs, Kalecki's fourth proposal would favour higher materials usage since higher costs would obtain, in absolute terms, a higher profit margin. From this point of view, Włodzimierz Brus' profits-related bonus scheme, and his proposed general reform of the incentives system undoubtedly has many advantages.[15] Such a bonus system would simultaneously encourage production, cost-effectiveness, and improved quality.

But Kalecki also saw disadvantages in paying bonuses out of profits. Among other consequences, this would lead to considerable variations in bonus payments, irrespective of the efforts of the workforce, as a result of differences in the technical conditions of production in different factories. In order to prevent this, a complicated system of adjustments to the formula relating bonuses to profits would be necessary (hence Kalecki's reservations about management by 'automatic incentives'). Moreover, although the payment of bonuses out of profits would encourage quantitative increases in production, differentiated margins would induce, at the same time, a tendency to manipulate the mix of final output in order to obtain higher margins. In order to avoid this, factory prices ought to be changed along with changes in the enterprises' own costs for each particular product mix. But the constant changes in price that this would imply would be very difficult to maintain. Paying profit-related bonuses would also not resolve the problem of quality, since in a situation of considerable excess demand, purchasers are unlikely to complain about defective articles. As for cost-effectiveness, this incentive would not operate selectively. (Whereas in certain cases it may be more important for the economy to increase production even at high costs, in others, cost-reduction may be desirable even if production does not rise.)

While seeing the advantages of a general reform in the system of incentives, based on profit-related bonuses which would radically simplify the whole system, Kalecki declared himself in favour of gradual improvements in the existing incentive system. This approach seemed to him to be 'probably the better alternative'.[16]

With his statements about material incentives, Kalecki entered into the mainstream of the Polish discussion on economic reform. Its most recent phase had started as early as the beginning of 1953, following the publication in the previous year of Joseph Stalin's *The Economic Problems of Socialism in the USSR*. Stalin's book broke the silence on the problems of economic management and policy development. The discussions around these issues were cast in the form of a debate on the role of the 'law of value' in a socialist economy. From the beginning of 1953, the view was increasingly expressed in Poland, for instance in the Party's theoretical journal *Nowe Drogi*, in *Ekonomista*, and in the serious press of the day, that 'insufficient allowance is made for the Law of Value in the organisation of the socialist economy'. Proposals for wider 'applications' of this law became an important theoretical premise behind proposed changes in economic management and policy-making, and a synonym for making greater use of market mechanisms in the economy.

Criticism of the existing system of planning and management, and the arbitrariness and excessive centralisation of economic decision-making, by theorists as well as by practitioners also entered into the discussion. Arguments for decentralisation were linked up with the arguments which had been behind the discussion in the 1930s of economic calculation under socialism. In effect, the suggestions that more scope should be given to the Law of Value were put together with, and were often identified with, proposals for economic decentralisation, by which was meant above all the extension of enterprise autonomy, and greater scope for market forces.

The chief spokesman on behalf of these reforms was Włodzimierz Brus. In articles published between 1953 and 1955, he argued for the need to guarantee a deciding role in fundamental economic policy-making for the central planner, while decentralising other economic decisions, and reforming the system of implementing the central plan in the direction of greater use of market mechanisms and limiting administrative co-ordination. Another economist, Henryk Fiszel also demanded 'greater scope' for the Law of Value in respect of prices, indicating that rational pricing was a general prerequisite for rational economic calculation.[17] However, the greatest publicity in these debates was gained by the many examples of the absurd extremes to which the centralisation of planning had been taken.[18]

It was in such an atmosphere that the above-mentioned conference on material incentives in a socialist economy took place. Kalecki's paper, which opened the conference, elicited much argument. Those who advocated an enhanced role for profits drew attention to the various problems which were bound to arise in implementing

Kalecki's piecemeal proposals. It was suggested therefore that instead of comparing what were essentially two different approaches to resolving the problem of economic incentives, by contrasting the advantages of one with the disadvantages of the other, the benefits and difficulties of each should be considered.

In the course of the discussion, Brus stated that

> the central problem of material incentives lies in linking them with the operation of the Law of Value in the economy as a whole. Limiting this problem to the distribution of bonuses in particular enterprises Professor Kalecki appears to have abstracted away from this broader set of issues. The extent of the influence of incentives is not confined to the bonus system, but also includes the accounting systems used in the economy, on which the relations between particular enterprises are based . . . The problem of integrating the general economic interest with material incentives at the enterprise level consists not only in mobilising productive reserves in enterprises, but also in making use of the reserves concealed throughout the economy as a whole.[19]

At this stage of the discussion, Kalecki did not regard any of these matters of principle, including the methods to be used in improving the effectiveness of economic incentives, as settled. In his opinion, they required further theoretical refinement and exchanges of views, since only thus could the best solution for the actual conditions in Poland at the time be arrived at.[20]

Notes

1. Kalecki published in *Przegląd Socjalistyczny* under the pseudonym Stanisław Braun.
2. Quoted in M. Kalecki, *Dzieła*, vol. I (Warsaw: Państwowe Wydawnictwo Ekonomiczne: PWE), pp. 434–5.
3. Ibid.
4. See O. Lange, *Dzieła* (Collected Works), vol. II (Warsaw: PWE, 1973), pp. 149–83, 534–46.
5. This was published in *Labour Discussion Notes*, no. 35 (September 1942).
6. Ibid.
7. Ibid. Kalecki however does not indicate what would determine the 'directness' of this control, nor how it would appear in the period of transition in a country such as Great Britain.

8. M. Kalecki, 'Workers Councils and Central Planning,' in *Selected Essays on Economic Planning* (Cambridge University Press, 1986).
9. M. Kalecki, *Dzieła*, vol III, p. 302.
10. Op. cit.
11. Z. Augustowski, 'Finansowanie aprowizacji reglamentowanej', *Spółdzielczy Przegląd Bankowy* (1946), nos. 15 and 16.
12. This is confirmed by the notes and memoranda found among Kalecki's own papers, and in the Archives of the Council of Ministers. See *Dzieł a*, vol. III.
13. See op. cit.
14. Op. cit., p. 87.
15. See W. Brus, *Prawo wartości a problematyka bodźców ekonomicznych* (Warsaw, 1956). For the definitive version of Professor Brus' proposed reform of economic planning, see *The Market in a Socialist Economy* (London, Routledge & Kegan Paul, 1972), ch. 5.
16. M. Kalecki, *Dzieła*, vol. III, p. 91.
17. See H. Fiszel, *Prawo wartości a problematyka cen w przemyśle socjalistycznym* (Warsaw, 1956). See also Z. Fedorowicz, *O prawie wartości i rozrachunku gospodarczym* (Warsaw, 1956).
18. See B. Minc, 'W sprawie metod planowania', *Trybuna Ludu* (20 March, 1956). The contributions of some of the other participants in this phase of the debate were collected and published in *Ekonomiści dyskutują prawo wartości* (Warsaw, 1956). The significance of this debate lay not so much in the views that were expressed in it – similar views had been propounded even earlier in Poland by, among others, Edward Taylor and Aleksy Wakar – but in the fact that this time many economists that were well connected with the central political and economic authorities expressed themselves in favour of the greater use of price and market mechanisms in the socialist economy.
19. Conference Materials in *Szkice Ekonomiczne*, Institute of Economics, Polish Academy of Sciences (Warsaw, 1958) vol. I, pp. 45–6.
20. M. Kalecki, *Dzieła*, vol. III, pp. 316–17.

2 The Question of Workers' Self-Management

THE RISE OF WORKERS' COUNCILS

From 1953, criticism of the centralised and bureaucratised Polish economic system became increasingly widespread in the ranks of the Government and Party administration and among economic managers and intellectuals. In this atmosphere pressure from management of industrial enterprises, supported by the conclusions of theoretical discussions on the need to decentralise the system of economic management gave rise to a joint resolution of the Central Committee of the Polish United Workers' Party (PUWP) and the Council of Ministers, on 9 April 1956, on extending the powers of directors of industrial enterprises.

At the time, this was known as the 'Director's Charter'. Had it appeared a few months earlier, it might have been recognised as the first step in the direction of rationalising and debureaucratising the economy. But, after the Twentieth Congress of the Communist Party of the Soviet Union in February 1956, which had a catalytic role in Poland, expectations had been raised and the resolution met with a somewhat critical and disappointed reaction.[1] In the press, criticism of economic absurdities and waste was taken up (especially in the weekly *Po Prostu*). A survey on 'How to rationalise the system of national economic management', conducted by the Party daily *Trybuna Ludu* at the end of May 1956 brought in hundreds of replies expressing above all the bitterness of frustrated hopes.

After the drastic reductions in real earnings in the years 1950–3, 1956 was supposed to see a further gradual elimination of disproportion in the economy, accompanied by real pay increases. But the contrast between the hardship and sacrifices endured by the population and the obvious waste of resources and energy, dimensions of which were now being revealed and which resulted from the bureaucratic and overcentralised system of economic management, more often than not contributed to the disintegration of political authority and increased social tension. Attempts to alleviate this by extending the powers of local government, on the one hand, and improvements in the material welfare of selected occupational groups, on the other, did not bring the results expected by the authorities. Declarations by factory workers that their efforts were wasted because of the errors of the bureaucratic system of economic management, became more frequent and critical in their tone, and their increasingly public demonstration was also partially reflected in the press. The central and local authorities were criticised for their tardiness in introducing the new principles of management which were supposed to enlarge enterprise autonomy and tie workers' earnings more clearly to their economic performance.

It was in this tense atmosphere that disturbances took place in Poznań on 28–29 April 1956. They were precipitated by an attempt to introduce in the L Cegielski engineering works new work norms that had been increased in proportion to increases in productivity, but leaving piece-rates unchanged. The new norms were based on principles that had already been criticised by Kalecki, among others, at a conference in the previous January of the Economics Institute of the Polish Academy of Sciences.[2] Shortly after the Poznań events, workers' councils and workshop committees started up spontaneously, initially in Poznań and Warsaw, and subsequently throughout the country.

Undoubtedly of major significance in determining this form of working-class economic democracy was the tradition of local and workers' self-government. From the turn of the century this had played a vital role in both the ideology and political programmes of Polish socialists and the history of the co-operative movement before the Second World War and during the Occupation. Immediately after the war, and without waiting for formal permission or statutes, workers themselves got production going, appointed their representative bodies and managed factories. It was only the later nationalisation measures that radically constrained workers' control and led to its obliteration.

Another factor may have been the example of Yugoslavia, although not much was known about it before the end of 1956, and later, for various reasons, this source of ideas about workers' self-management was not acknowledged. Nevertheless, in the middle of 1956, Czesław Bobrowski's book *Socialist Yugoslavia* was translated into Polish and circulated for the internal use of the staff of the Polish National Bank.[3] This argued in favour of decentralisation and pointed to the advantages of the Yugoslav system of workers' control. At the same time, Artur Hajnicz published in *Życie Warszawy* (the Warsaw daily newspaper) a series of reports about his visit to Yugoslavia with other Party journalists from Poland. While pointing out certain weaknesses in the Yugoslav system which did not solve broader problems of political democracy, he came out decidedly in support of decentralisation and workers' control, seeing in them a way of resolving the problem of socialist ownership.

Finally, according to Hajnicz's later (unpublished) recollections, a small group of journalists, writers and Party activists played a part in initiating the workers' council movement in Warsaw. From late spring 1956 they met regularly and discussed various proposals for changes in economic management, methods of exerting pressure on the authorities, and ways of starting up the workers' control movement.[4]

In many factories workers and the newly-formed workers' councils demanded greater enterprise autonomy and asked that their enterprises be allowed to undertake so-called 'economic experiments'.[5] The spontaneity of this movement and the speed with which it spread, as well as the radical form which these demands sometimes took (and the way in which on occasion accounts were settled with enterprise bosses for their economic mismanagement) did not make it easy for the authorities to adopt a consistent attitude towards it. The prevailing reaction was a tendency to take over the movement and gain control of it. However, attempts to neutralise it by a further extension of local government powers (in June and July 1956), and promises to extend the powers of the trades unions' works committees (at the end of August) were not successful.

In this situation a special Commission to Assist the Proper Development of Workers' Initiatives in Workplace Management (*Komisja dla Okazania Pomocy we Właściwym Rozwijaniu Inicjatywy Załóg w Dziedzinie Zarządzania Zakładami*), was appointed 'to control the spontaneity of the process and channel it in the appropriate directions'.[6] The chairman of this commission was Vice-Premier Piotr Jaroszewicz, hence it became widely known as the Jaroszewicz Commission. His vice chairmen were the Minister for the Machine Industry, Bolesław Jaszczuk, and an 'adviser to the Council of Ministers', Michał Kalecki. Among the twenty-eight members of this commission were two university economists, Włodzimierz Brus and Edward Lipiński, eight directors of large industrial enterprises, six economic ministers or their deputies, two heads of departments of the Central Committee of the PUWP, the Secretary of the Warsaw Party Committee, and two secretaries of the Party's factory branches. This membership was supposed to ensure a consensus between economic theoreticians and practitioners from different levels, with a clear preponderance of the latter.

THE WORK OF THE JAROSZEWICZ COMMISSION

Even before the commission was set up, Kalecki drew attention to the fact that the setting up of workers' councils was a very important development, but one that produced complicated problems in reconciling the particular interests of an enterprise's workforce with the overall social interest. A few days later, at the first meeting of the commission, he made the following statement.

> It seems to me that in this discussion two kinds of reform in enterprise management are advanced. First there is the question of workers' control of the enterprise. Secondly, there is the issue of greater enterprise autonomy in the context of central planning and the related issue of material incentives.
>
> Workers' self-management depends on a further extension of enterprise autonomy and the material interest of the workforce. But these questions are not strictly linked with each other in the sense that setting up workers' self-management does not depend on how much autonomy is granted to enterprises and what form it takes, nor on the system of material incentives that will be established for the workforce. It is therefore possible to work out general principles for organising workers' control without deciding in advance the scope of central planning and the system of material incentives. Hence I support the proposal of my colleague Professor Brus to start with a general statute for workers' councils independently of the economic issues (associated with extending enterprise autonomy) even though the economy will progress in this direction.
>
> The second question is more complicated. How is it possible to reconcile in theory and in practice the extension of enterprise autonomy with the fully maintained system of central planning on which we all agree? And how difficult the matter of setting material incentives is! First of all, it depends on the conditions in which those incentives will operate, and thus on the setting of appropriate

> prices. The discussion has clearly shown that the attempt to find a universal model of future solutions is infeasible: they must be adapted to the conditions in particular branches of industry and even in particular enterprises.
>
> There is yet another issue which has arisen in the discussion and which I would like to emphasise. Extending an enterprise's autonomy and making its operation more efficient do not necessarily lead to beneficial results for the enterprise, and for the economy as a whole. Results that are advantageous for the enterprise need not necessarily be advantageous for the whole economy.[7]

In Kalecki's opinion, conflicts of interest could arise above all in the areas of employment, investment and foreign trade. If the main constraint imposed on the enterprise is the total wage bill alone, the profit-maximising enterprise will tend to contract employment. Absorbing the resulting unemployment by a general expansion of production (given the existing constraints on raw materials supplies) would not be at all easy. Nevertheless, Kalecki pointed out, in a socialist country someone must take care of the unemployed.

Regarding investment, on the one hand, from the point of view of the enterprise, it would suit the enterprise best if it disposed freely of its investment fund, gross of amortisation. On the other hand, total investment is limited not just by inflationary pressures, but also by material constraints. Within the framework of the total investment fund, the most effective investments and the optimal structure of foreign trade should be determined so as to achieve the highest possible growth in supplies, production, and living standards. Thus in the case of investment too it was necessary to find the best possible compromise. Kalecki foresaw similar difficulties arising in relation to foreign trade. Because of these complications he considered that the proposed reforms should not be introduced at once and simultaneously in all enterprises.

During the next two weeks, a working group directed by Kalecki prepared proposals for three basic laws on extending the autonomy of industrial enterprises, on workers' councils and on the enterprise fund. The greatest disputes within the group arose in the discussions on the extension of enterprise autonomy. Because of his experience of pre-war Poland, and of the developed capitalist countries after the war, Kalecki was very sensitive to the question of full employment. However, other members of the group were of the opinion that the basic constraint imposed on the individual enterprise by the central plan ought simply to be the total wages bill. They assumed that if enterprise management could reduce employment, then the average wage would rise, but so also would labour productivity. Similar opinions and attitudes prevailed among the management of many factories.

This solution did not satisfy Kalecki. He feared that it could become an additional source of unemployment in Poland. In his view, the size of the total labour force in an enterprise ought also to be set for it by the authorities. It is worth citing his bitter and ironic observation on this dispute: 'In England for so long I was paid to work on eliminating unemployment. Now you want to pay me to create it!'

In practice, the question of large-scale redundancies in enterprises did not arise. The tradition of over-manning, the opposition of trades unions to attempts to reduce employment, but above all the absence of any more radical changes in the direction of making enterprises more fully responsive to market pressures, meant that Kalecki's fears turned out to be groundless.[8]

These three acts of legislation constituted an organic whole. Their essential characteristics were their recognition of workers' councils as the leading agency of enterprise management, and some relaxation of the centralised allocation of resources. Both of these features reflected the climate of opinion at the time, and the views of Kalecki, who had a definite and radical conception of the place and role of workers' self-management, one that was in fact little different from that which he had expressed in 1942 (see Chapter 1).

The extension of enterprise autonomy created the opportunity for workers' councils to decide the pattern and organisation of production, while the law on enterprise funds created the material incentive to take advantage of these new powers to improve the economic efficiency of the enterprise. However, the central plan still laid down the most important indicators of economic performance by enterprises, in particular the value of their marketed output, the amount produced of the most important items, and their total wages bills. While replacement investment was decentralised, decisions about the construction of new projects remained in the hands of the central planners. Prices were to continue to be fixed centrally, and essential materials and semi-manufactured goods were to continue to be distributed according to priorities determined by the central authorities. Foreign trade was also to be entirely centrally controlled.

This meant that despite an extension of the domain of commodity/money relations in the economy, it retained the essential characteristics of a quasi-money economy.

WORKERS' COUNCILS AND CENTRAL PLANNING

The essence of the economic system that emerged as a result of the spontaneous rise of workers' councils, was that it created the possibility of enterprise management by workers' councils operating within the framework of central planners' directives. Realising full well the difficulties of reconciling workers' councils and central planning, Kalecki sought to answer two questions; First, is such a combination desirable from the social and economic point of view and, secondly, is it viable in the long run?

Kalecki had no doubts in answering the first of these questions. He considered the new system of management to be desirable above all because its component elements, that is directive central planning and workers' councils, were indispensable for securing rapid economic development, but free from the distortions that had characterised the previous system. Eliminating these distortions would be guaranteed by the existence of the workers' councils, which would carry out the following functions:

1. As an authority directly responsible to the workforce, they would prevent abuses of conditions of work and overtime payments, and similar impositions of past years.
2. They would counteract the tendency towards excessive bureaucratisation and centralisation of the economy, since their resistance to this would be far more effective than that of enterprise directors who owe their appointment to the central authorities.
3. Finally, given the appropriate material incentives, their close contact with the workforce would release initiative which it is impossible to inspire by central planning.[9]

At the same time, Kalecki resolutely defended central planning by directives with the broad scope described above. He considered the proposal, often advanced at that time in Poland, to replace central planning by a system of incentives which would induce the enterprise to make the maximum possible use of its productive capacity, as inappropriate and unrealistic. This was because, first of all, allowances would have to be made for differences in the profit share distributed to workers in different plants due to varying degrees of technological backwardness between plants. Apart from the arbitrariness of any assessment of relative technological disadvantage, there would be considerable practical difficulties in allowing for it. This is because the ratio of profits to wages would be constantly changing, while social justice would require continuous modifications in the system of compensation for technical backwardness. Secondly, the incentives to be derived from profit shares would be quite limited. If income from this source were set at a high level relative to basic pay, then significant and undesirable fluctuations in workers' incomes might occur. However, if the share of profits distributed to workers did not constitute a significant part of their income, then its effect on the economic efficiency of the enterprise would be small. Thirdly, profit-related bonuses would be conducive not only to increased production, but to cost-cutting as well, especially by reducing employment. The latter could be socially undesirable.

In Kalecki's opinion, all these drawbacks of profit-sharing arose from the very essence of socialism, namely that it aims at improving as much as possible the living standards of the broad mass of the population, and not profit-maximisation.

As for the other elements of directive central planning, leaving prices to be determined by 'free market forces' would be equivalent to setting prices on the basis of tacit or overt agreements between enterprises. This would indeed be the easiest way of achieving high profits, though thereby inhibiting rather than expanding production.

Kalecki also viewed the proposals to replace the administrative allocation of materials by a flexible pricing policy exercised by the central authorities, as unrealistic. He pointed out that even in developed capitalist countries where surplus capacity normally exists, in situations in which the price mechanism breaks down, due to acute shortages of basic commodities (for example, during the Second World War, or even during the period of rapid rearmament in 1950–3), their governments also resorted to administrative rationing of materials according to their own priorities.

These arguments convinced Kalecki that a synthesis of workers' councils and central planning was desirable in all respects. But this still did not prejudge the issue of whether such a system was likely to last. Kalecki warned against the illusion that it would be free of contradictions and easy to manage. He had no doubt that there would always be tendencies in it to increase centralisation at the expense of the rights of workers' councils, as well as counter-tendencies to diminish the role of the central plan by the actions of the councils:

> On the one hand there will exist the danger of weakening the position of the workers' councils and bureaucratising the whole system of management. On the other hand, pressure from the workers' councils may lead to a situation in which it will be necessary either to slow the pace of economic development or to make this development dependent on foreign aid. Alternatively, after a period of chaos 'order' will be restored with a return to a system of bureaucratic centralism.[10]

At all costs, Kalecki thought, a balance between these conflicting tendencies needed to be achieved and maintained.

WORKERS' COUNCILS AND CENTRAL ADMINISTRATION

The laws proposed by the Jaroszewicz Commission were already prepared before the VIII Plenum of the Central Committee of the PUWP (19–21 October 1956) and the return to power of Władyslaw Gomułka. Their approval by the Sejm (the Polish Parliament) reflected the aspirations of factory workers and some Party intellectuals for radical change, rather than the intentions of Gomułka himself and the central Party administration. During the discussions at the Plenum the question of workers' councils was not settled. Gomułka neither clearly supported them, nor did he decide in favour of their institutionalisation. Instead he merely addressed this topic with a few generalisations. The same was true of the majority of the other speakers. The councils were only supported by Piotr Jaroszewicz, and the chairman of the State Commission for Economic Planning, Eugeniusz Szyr.

In Jaroszewicz's view, the setting up of workers' councils was one of the essential requirements for overcoming the country's economic difficulties. 'Any curbing of this mass movement', he said, 'would have the most adverse repercussions on expanding production, on the extension of political and economic initiative among the workers, and on the process of building a socialist society.'[11] He thought that the Plenum should adopt a resolution supporting workers' self-management in the form of workers' councils, and emphasising that 'what we are doing does not constitute the conclusion, but merely the start of management reforms and of the development of workers' democracy in factories'.[12]

This declaration was partially reflected in the Plenum resolution which, on the question of the economic function of workers' self-management, went much further than Gomułka's speech. It repudiated the resolution passed by the previous Plenum, which supported extending the rights of the trades' unions' works committees. The VIII Plenum resolution defined the power of workers' councils' and anticipated the introduction of workers' self-management, first in those enterprises most prepared for it, and subsequently in all other enterprises.[13]

Eugeniusz Szyr criticised the draft of the Plenum's political resolution for separating the question of workers' councils from that of the new role of the Sejm. In doing so, he pondered on the need to create a co-ordinating organisation for workers' councils.' Up to now, he argued,

> the enterprise has been regarded as merely a link in the general system of state ownership. Now we wonder whether we ought not to see the working class as simultaneously a direct co-owner and manager of socialised means of production. A discussion along these lines . . . would give rise to a belief in the efficacy of integrating workers' councils at the city, district, regional and country-wide levels, and thus also would lead to the notion of workers' council representation in the Sejm.[14]

Neither the resolution of the VIII Plenum of the Central Committee, nor an article by J Wacławek under the significant headline 'For Workers' Self-management' which appeared in the Party daily *Trybuna Ludu* shortly before the Plenum met, dispersed the distrust and indecision in the central Party apparatus and the state administration. A few month's later, in mid-February 1957, a resolution of the Party activists from the thirty largest industrial plants in Warsaw called upon the central leadership of the Party to provide decisive support for the workers' councils.[15]

Meanwhile, the workers' council movement was spreading. According to estimates made by the Polish press agency, PAP, by the end of January 1957, 500 workers' councils had been established in industry. In Silesia there were around 200 councils, in Łódź, the second largest Polish city, there were 40, and in Warsaw there were workers' councils in the majority of key industrial plants. Nearly half of the enterprises in the chemicals industry had elected workers' councils, and councils operated in all shipyards and around three-quarters of mines.

According to later data supplied by the Instytut Gospodarstwa Społecznego (the Polish Institute for Social and Economic Research), based on information from the Polish trades union confederation, the Centralna Rada Związków Zawodowych (the Central Council of Trades Unions), at the end of 1957, there were in Poland over 5600 workers' councils. In relation to the number of factories in which they could have operated, this amounted to around 50 per cent of that number, compared with 26 per cent in mid-1957. This proportion was higher in the larger factories: workers' councils arose primarily in the large industrial agglomerations. They were therefore becoming an important form of working-class organisation in larger productive units. The proportion of manual workers in the councils was 55 per cent, while in the councils' executives, this proportion was 42 per cent. The percentage of council members who were also members of the PUWP was around 40 per cent, while in council executives, their share was 48 per cent.

In an assessment by the Economic Council of the impact of the law on workers' councils, it was pointed out that in their first year of existence, the councils had already played a positive role. This was not just in the socio-political aspects of their activity, but also directly, in helping to overcome many of the current economic difficulties. After an initial period of organisation, the majority of councils concentrated their attention on the economic problems of their enterprises, such as increasing production, reducing costs, improving labour productivity and so on.

Some councils took up longer-term issues, such as the introduction of new ways of organising production, introducing departmental accounting systems, setting up the manufacture of new products, changes in the product mix, modifications in the pay structure, setting up special working groups for economic analyses, and so on. The councils also took initiatives on more general matters, such as combating absenteeism, and the decline in work discipline. In general, the Economic Council thought that the workers' councils achieved considerable results in bringing some order to the economy. Their establishment released initiative in places of work, while the activity of workers' councils was greatly assisted by material incentives in the form of workers' profit-sharing.

The councils nevertheless met with numerous obstacles to their activities. As time went on, these activities diminished. Among other reasons, this was because of changes in their composition at the beginning of 1957, brought about as a result of new or supplementary elections to the councils, in which attempts were made to eliminate the influence of particularly active advocates of workers' control. Furthermore, there was a lack of direction about what they should be doing in the longer term. There was also insufficient support for the idea of workers' self-management in the official press and the mass media.

But the basic causes of their difficulties lay elsewhere. First of all the councils had to operate in a virtually unchanged system of economic management. No radical reform of prices, which would have enabled autonomous enterprises to perform according to more rational economic calculation,[16] was carried out. The system of planning also remained unreconstructed in the direction of a wider use of parametric (price-type) indicators in place of administrative directives. Enterprises continued to be subordinated to central boards (subsequently industrial associations), and economic ministries. Obviously in such a situation there was little room for enterprise autonomy. Yet without it, as Oskar Lange had earlier pointed out,

> workers' and employee's councils would be a fiction, since they would have nothing on which to decide . . . The latter requires enterprises, and consequently the whole economy, to move away from management based on administrative commands to management based on the expert use of economic incentives and the social responsibility of workers.[17]

However, no such basic reform was carried out.

A second and even more fundamental cause of problems was the ambiguous attitude of the Party, Government, and trades union leaderships to the nature and importance of the workers' council movement. The majority of the central authorities sought to neutralise the movement and recover control over the situation in the enterprises. Some came out in support of some extension of enterprise autonomy, seeing in that a condition for improving the economic efficiency. Others advocated workers' self-management in economic matters, but opposed the political tendencies of the movement. There were also a few who considered that this form of direct workers' democracy was perhaps even more important at the time than the return of the Sejm to its proper role. (During the

Stalinist period, it had degenerated into a mere organ of acclamation for Government and Party decisions.)

In the central Party apparatus, it was primarily the young secretaries to the Central Committee, such as Jerzy Albrecht, Jerzy Morawski, Władysław Matwin, the head of the Central Committee's Economic Department, Józef Olszewski, and, later on, Roman Zambrowski, who supported the workers' council movement. However, many did not have a developed opinion on the issue, so if at the end of 1956 the workers' council movement had established itself, this was primarily due to the fact that it had already achieved some momentum, and actual political circumstances dictated a particular organisational development.

What were the main reasons for the opposition of that part of the Party and Government leadership that remained hostile to workers' councils? First, workers' councils were chosen by their workforces in genuinely democratic elections. In many councils the most important, or among the most important, influences were wielded by technicians and engineers, often non-Party members. The councils were therefore not open to manipulation by the authorities. Secondly, the councils were more active in many matters (especially in the initial stages of their existence) than the factory committees of the Party or trades unions. This is what often lay behind accusations that the councils were duplicating the activities of these committees. A third factor, and the one arousing perhaps the greatest opposition, was the idea already mentioned, of vertically-integrated workers' councils, set up not just at the factory level but also at higher levels in the economic administration. There were suggestions that they should have some role in the structure of local government and should even be represented in the Sejm.

Kalecki supported this idea to some extent. He considered that in the economic administration and industrial associations enterprises should be represented not just by their directors, but also by delegates from their workers' councils. He thought that such representation of the councils would strengthen the links between the enterprises and their supervising agencies, and would thus facilitate the management of enterprises. Workers' councils would then orientate themselves to what was going on in the agencies in charge of enterprises and, in a sense, would become co-responsible for the decisions taken there.[18]

On the other hand, the vertical integration of workers' councils inspired fears that they would transform themselves into political organisations that would introduce elements of pluralism into the political and institutional structure of the country. It seems that such fears determined the ultimate fate of the councils.

The way in which these fears and problems were resolved by decisively rejecting the notion of a horizontal structure for the councils, was already anticipated in a speech by Władysław Gomułka at the IX Plenum of the Central Commiteee of the PUWP in May 1957. There he said:

> Others demand that workers' councils should be set up not only in places of work, but also extended vertically above the factory level, according to industry. This notion assumes the dissolution of enterprise central boards as managing agencies in the economy . . . Workers' councils built up vertically . . . would need to be subordinate to some central authority. Should it be the Government? The Government could not be the superior authority for the type of social organisations that workers' councils are . . . The whole idea (of vertical structures) leads nowhere . . . In short, in the whole of this notion is revealed an anarchist utopia . . . The development of the workers' council movement and their activity can in the future find different ways of extending the influence of the councils on the economy. However, at present the councils cannot be left to their own fate, just as they cannot be deprived of their independent and self-managing character. In the present situation, the only real way of giving workers' councils the organisation and other help that they require is to entrust these tasks to the trades unions . . . The need has arisen to link up workers' councils with the trades unions in such a way that does not alter the autonomous character of the councils and their independence of the unions . . . Party members who are also members of councils should be organised in Party caucuses, with which the local leadership of the Party should systematically co-operate.[19]

The following months witnessed an abundance of meetings and conferences devoted above all to the relations between workers' councils, enterprise directors, and the factory organisations of the Party and trades unions. From the beginning of 1958, they were accompanied by experimental associations of workers' councils and the factory committees of the Party and trades unions in one overall organisation. From the start this placed the workers' councils at a disadvantage in relation to their other partners, representing hierarchically structured, and hence stronger, organisations.

At the IV Congress of Trades Unions in May 1958, Władysław Gomułka proposed the setting up in enterprises of Workers' Control Conferences (Konferencje Samorządu Robotniczego, or KSR for short), which would be composed of all the members of workers' councils and the factory committees of the Party and trades unions respectively.[20] After a few months of further discussion and experiments, on 21 December 1958 the Sejm accepted legislation which re-organised workers' self-management and set up Workers' Control Conferences.

Thus in Poland there prevailed a view, in large part due to Kalecki's efforts, that it was necessary to reconcile workers' self-management with central planning. This was in contrast to the Yugoslav notion of highly decentralised self-management, leaving little scope for central planning. In pointing to the basis of the contradictions between workers' councils and central planning, Kalecki took up a problem of critical significance for the future of both these institutions. However, there was not enough time to see if they could be made compatible with each other. Before a new system of economic organisation combining workers' councils with central planning could be tested, the councils were submerged in broader institutions and subordinated to the Party apparatus.

In practice, this solution led to the elimination of pluralist authority in enterprises, and a return to the manipulation of the councils. It removed the threat to the system of political authority that might have emerged from vertical integration of the representation of workers' self-management outside the enterprises. After a few years, the workers' self-management thus reorganised lost its practical significance; Party committees in the factories went back to administering them from day to day while factory councils ceased their independent activity. Workers' councils were finally abolished in 1979, but the superficial character of the Workers' Control Conferences had already effectively discouraged workers from participation in such self-management.

Notes

1. See for example 'Dyskusja z dyrektorami warszawskich fabryk' ('Discussion with the Directors of Warsaw Factories'), *Nowe Drogi* (1967), no. 4, pp. 54–61.

2. See p. 13.
3. A little earlier, extensive fragments of this book were circulated internally by the Polish Institute of International Affairs (*Polski Instytut Spraw Międzynarodowych* – PISM), and it was eventually published in Warsaw in 1957.
4. Cf T. Kowalik 'Spory o ustrój społeczno-gospodarczy Polski 1948–1958' (Debates on the socio-economic system of Poland 1948–1958), unpublished typescript. See also the series of articles by B. N. Łopieńska and E. Szymańska, 'Ludzie z *Po Prostu*' (The People from *Po Prostu*), *Kultura* (1981).
5. For an outline of these experiments, see *Dzieła*, vol. III, pp. 351–2.
6. See *Zarządzenie Prezesa Rady Ministrów z dnia 2 października 1956 r.* Archiwum URM ref. 547/5.
7. Proceedings of the commission's first sitting, quoted in M. Kalecki, *Dzieła*, vol. III, pp. 321–2.
8. Kalecki was not alone in these fears. They were shared by, among others Hilary Minc (by then in retirement), who somewhat later, but in a similar context criticised the economic plan for 1961–5, on the grounds that its implementation would create unemployment in Poland.
9. M. Kalecki, 'Workers' Councils and Central Planning', in *Selected Essays on Economic Planning*.
10. Ibid., p. 99.
11. *Nowe Drogi* (1956), No. 10, p. 52.
12. Ibid., p. 55.
13. Ibid., p. 6.
14. Ibid., p. 258. This proposal not only did not find its way into the final resolution passed by the Plenum, but at the next plenary session of the Central Committee was already opposed as an anarchist utopia.
15. See *Trybuna Ludu*, 12 February 1957.
16. As long as the administrative allocation of resources is maintained, economic calculation is more concerned with the fulfilment of plan indicators than with the relationship between inputs and outputs. Thus there was no question of making economic calculation *completely* rational within the new system of economic management in Poland at the time.
17. O. Lange, *Dzieła*, Vol. II (Warsaw, 1973), pp. 475–6.
18. M. Kalecki, *Dzieła*, vol III, pp. 331 and 359. For the attitude of the Economic Council towards the vertical integration of workers' councils, see ch. 3, n. 18 below.
19. W. Gomułka, 'Węzłowe problemy polityki partii' ('Central Policy Issues of the Party'), *Trybuna Ludu*, 16 May 1957.
20. See *Trybuna Ludu*, 16 May 1958. Gomułka entrusted the preparation of KSR legislation to the Central Council of Trades Unions, and not to the central party administration. Unlike the leadership of the Trades Union Council, the latter had not expressed such unambiguous opposition to workers' councils.

3 The Functioning of the Socialist Economy

THE MODEL PROPOSED BY THE ECONOMIC COUNCIL

At the Second Congress of Polish Economists held on 7–9 June 1956, Piotr Ehrlich proposed the creation of an advisory government agency, which would be composed of independent economists. The job of this proposed Economic Council would be the expert assessment of government regulations and economic policy, as well as putting forward its own proposals in this area of policy. At the same time, the drawing up and putting forward for public discussion of reports on the state of the economy and the fundamental principles of economic reforms was to be the task of a Social Survey Commission that would be independent of the government. The linking of the proposal to set up this Commission to a vote of no confidence in the economic leadership made the fate of this suggestion a foregone conclusion. After the Economists' Congress, the expectations that had been invested in the Survey Commission were transferred to the Economic Council.

The responsibility for carrying out Congress resolutions fell on the leadership of the Polish Economic Association. They, and subsequently also the government, delayed the appointment of the Council. The work of organising it was started in September, only to be broken off in October by the events which culminated in the return to power of Gomułka at the VIII Plenary Session of the Central Committee. The Economic Council of the Council of Ministers was finally constituted on 1 December 1956. Its chairman was Oskar Lange, and its full-time acting deputy chairman was Czesław Bobrowski. Kalecki was one of the other five deputy chairmen of the Council.

Three main tasks dominated the programme of the Economic Council. First of all, it drafted changes in the system of planning and economic management, and thus elaborated the concept of the 'Polish model' for the organisation of a socialist economy. Secondly, it examined economic plans and current economic policies. Finally it was an important source of information: carrying out and publishing periodic assessments of the economic situation in the country and initiating research conducted further by other institutions.

In line with his earlier pronouncements Kalecki from the start, in Council discussions on the Polish economic 'model', came out against any single panacea for all economic ills. He was also against the mechanical replacement of all administrative directives by market-type incentives. Instead he favoured a balanced combination of incentives and directives. He considered that limiting central planning to giving only overall guidance could lead to even more serious mistakes than the detailed planning hitherto applied. He argued against allowing enterprises, except for a few small ones selling only to local markets, to set their own prices. He pointed out that the advocates of market mechanisms did not take into account the fact that market-type incentives based on cost calculations had only limited effect in expanding output. This was because, among other reasons, in the capitalist market economies on which the functioning of these incentives was modelled, there are reserves of productive capacity and stocks. However, in Poland there were no significant reserves of productive capacity. As a rule, therefore, increased production was only possible in the short run as a result of investment and increased employment.[1]

As for the difficulties and distortions revealed by the Six Year Plan (1950–5), these mainly arose, in his opinion, out of the substance of the Plan and its subsequent amendment, and not from the system of economic management. He saw the fundamental errors embodied in that plan and its fulfilment as:

(1) An excessive level of investment which, despite an unanticipated rise in defence expenditure, was not reduced in the course of the Plan's fulfilment;
(2) an over-emphasis on the construction of new plants and factories in relation to the improvement of already existing productive capacity;
(3) starting investment projects without prior and appropriate cost-benefit analysis;
(4) unjustified optimism in forecasting agricultural output and export markets; and
(5) the lengthening of the working week in coal-mining which, though of crucial significance for the export drive, exacerbated the labour shortages already existing in the industry.

> These errors [wrote Kalecki] were not so much the results of the way in which enterprises were managed as the cause of the extreme bureaucratisation and centralisation of that system. The acute disproportions that arose in the economy required increasingly extensive development of the administrative apparatus in order to rectify them. Obviously, once created, the apparatus tended to expand spontaneously. It is also clear that the consequences of such economic management exacerbated further the difficulties arising from the fundamental mistakes in planning.[2]

Like many reformist economists of that time, Kalecki saw mistakes in economic policy, and not the characteristics of the system of economic organisation, as the basic cause of the problems. In accordance with this broader view (which, we should note, Kalecki started to revise only in the 1960s), he did not underestimate the significance of changes in the system of enterprise management, but neither did he expect very much of them.

Kalecki maintained this attitude during the discussions on the Model Proposals in the Economic Council. At the third plenary session of the Council, on 11 May 1957, he stated, *inter alia*:

> The previous period was characterised by a dogmatic faith in the effectiveness of directives. As we know, this gave lamentable results. At the same time, these results themselves were illusory, since many directives were merely an incentive to evade them. Personally I am against all dogma and therefore I would not want this document to express exaggerated enthusiasm for incentives. Incentives are as yet untried, while directives, as we know from experience, did not give the right results. Because of this, I believe that we should attempt to obtain an optimal combination of incentives and directives.
>
> If anyone thinks that the administration of incentives will not require bureaucracy, that person is wrong. Incentives will need to be varied according to industrial peculiarities, and this will require a bureaucratic apparatus. I do not want this document to support any utopias or illusions, and because of that I consider that the best approach would be a consistent combination of directives and incentives.[3]

Further on in the discussion around the *Model Proposals*, Kalecki tried to put forward an outline of the implied way in which socialist enterprises should operate. He saw it as follows: the enterprise would receive a directive giving the level of its net output. This indicator would link up the enterprise's production with the central plan. The enterprise's wages bill would be fixed in relation to its net output. If, for example, net output was 10 per cent greater or less than planned, then the wages fund would change in the same proportion. Profit, that is, the difference between net output and the wages fund, would also vary in proportion to net output. In this way the decisive issue in the enterprise's production plan and its expenditure would be its net output. Increases in this output over a year or two would determine payments of bonsues out of profits.

This arrangement ensured consistency of incentives at the enterprise level, linking financial benefits not with the current level of net output, but with its continuous growth. If an enterprise were to rest on its laurels instead of improving its performance, then it would not gain any benefits.

Kalecki also advocated the representation of workers' councils on the boards of enterprise associations, supervising enterprise activity. But he considered that these associations should not be too large. He warned that if they embraced all enterprises in an industry, then the representatives of the enterprises in that industry would seek to obtain the greatest possible allocations of resources, reductions in quality, higher prices and so on. In his opinion, it was these monopolistic tendencies that ought to be resisted, rather than the direct representation of workers' councils on the boards of enterprise associations.[4]

Regardless of Kalecki's qualifications, the *Model Proposals* put forward a system of organising enterprise activity that was broadly in line with his suggestions presented above. Its basis was the coordination of autonomous and self-managing enterprises with the central plan by means of directive indicators of net output, and a few other such indicators. The net output indicator was, in turn, related to the wage fund and profit-sharing at the enterprise level, ensuring the system's consistency at micro level.

The Proposals Concerning the Directions of Reform in the Economic Model (the *Model Proposals*), accepted by the Economic Council, were the outcome of many compromises and did not put forward really radical measures. This was in part due to the composition of the Council, where a major role was played by the representatives of the central authorities, who promoted a generally conservative view. But it was also because some members of the Council realised that the economic reform would be introduced under unfavourable economic circumstances, with no reserves, so that many detailed provisions had to be accepted as the second-best but only obtainable solutions.

While the *Model Proposals* postulated a general project of long-term reform, only a few key problems were discussed in detail. The remainder were left to be resolved later, after the proposals had been accepted by the Government. Nevertheless, and despite clear omissions from them (for instance, regarding agriculture and foreign trade), the *Model Proposals* did provide a framework for a complex and internally consistent set of economic reforms. They also put forward a timetable for the introduction of specific changes, the aim of which was to accelerate the reconstruction of the system of managing the Polish economy.

There were two guiding principles underlying the *Model Proposals*. One was the replacement of administrative instruments for enterprise management by economic instruments and economic calculation (taking into account the specific circumstances of each industry). The other was the democratisation of the economy. This was to be achieved by the broad participation of workers, workers' councils, local authorities and the Sejm in the drawing up of economic plans and the setting of socio-economic goals. A necessary condition for this democratisation was to be openness of economic decision-making, and the formulation of the plan in such a way that the authorities and society at large should be fully aware of the alternatives from which economic choices were selected.

The acceptance of the *Model Proposals* would not only guide the future work of the Economic Council, but would also have significant implications for the rest of the economic reform movement. Therefore, as soon as they had been accepted by the Economic Model Commission, they were put forward for Government approval and made public.[5] After a delay of a month, the Government passed them over to the Economic Committee of the Council of Ministers, which postponed discussion of them for a further month.

Meanwhile, the *Model Proposals* were sharply criticised at a meeting of the Board of the Planning Commission. They were denounced as vague, tending to undermine (or at least seriously limit) the directive nature of central plans, accepting capitalist principles of enterprise management, difficult to implement because of the limited possibilities of radical price reforms, and so on.[6]

Similar objections to the *Model Proposals* were raised at the meeting of the Economic Committee of the Council of Ministers, where Czesław Bobrowski, Włodzimierz Brus, Oskar Lange and Kalecki gave further explanations and replied to this criticism.[7] The information released after this meeting in the weekly *Życie Gospodarcze*, which strongly supported reforms, was ostensibly favourable, indicating that the Economic Committee of Ministers approved the *Model Proposals* in principle as an outline of future economic reforms. However, according to Czesław Bobrowski, the then Prime Minister Józef Cyrankiewicz commented tersely after the meeting that the Committee neither accepted nor rejected the proposals.[8] A detailed analysis of the discussion at that meeting shows that the proposals were received in this way not because they were defective, but primarily because the reforms embodied in them were regarded as too radical.

This was an important set-back from the point of view of further work on economic reforms. If the *Model Proposals* had been accepted, albeit with some amendment, or rejected in favour of some other proposals, an economic reform might still have been carried through consistently and comprehensively, rather than in a fragmentary and haphazard way. This response also weakened the inspirational role of the *Model Proposals*, since their failure to obtain government approval was widely seen as expressing reservations on the part of the central authorities. There soon followed decisions whose substance and manner of preparation clearly indicated that the authorities had no intention of asking the Economic Council to complete or revise its proposed economic reforms, nor of being guided in their actions by them.

Thus the basis of the economic reforms that were actually undertaken remained the Council of Ministers' Resolution 704, extending the autonomy of industrial enterprises in the state sector (passed 10 November 1956), the Law on Workers' Councils and the 1957 Factory Fund Law. These were supplemented by corresponding changes in the regulations concerning plan methodology and management incentives in state enterprises.[9]

The *Model Proposals* suggested further reductions in the number of directive plan indicators, compared with the number postulated in Resolution 704. In practice, however, the course of events reversed this. Soon after Resolution 704 was passed, ministries and the boards of industrial associations started to impose on enterprises additional 'advisory' plan indicators that were not provided for in the resolution. The *Model Proposals* recommended a progressive reduction in the central rationing of raw materials and semi-fabricates. Any possibility of achieving this was severely compromised by over-ambitious plans and the resulting supply shortages. The proposed new principles of industrial organisation (see below, pp. 45–9) also failed to be implemented, and the new enterprise associations turned out in practice to be little different from the old Central Boards.

In plan methodology, the *Model Proposals* demanded more thorough economic analysis, the study of alternative plan variants, the subordination of short-term operative plans to long-term ones, and so on. Here too, little progress was made in practice. In the Planning Commission, a scheme of cost-benefit analysis for investment projects was worked out under Kalecki's direction. However, obliging investing enterprises to apply it (and, by implication, obliging them to prepare alternative schemes of investment to achieve a specified output target) proved in practice to be impossible. The idea of preparing alternative plan variants was rejected by the directorate of the Planning Commission.[10] All in all, despite a temporary reduction in the arbitrariness of economic planning, its essential principles remained unchanged.

In this situation, the remaining recommendation of the *Model Proposals* were left in an inauspicious void. The proposed new system of economic management was based on two pillars: enterprise autonomy and workers' self-management. But enterprises which in practice enjoyed little autonomy neither could nor wanted to operate economic calculation. Restrictions on the activities of workers' councils similarly weakened the second basis of the *Model Proposals*. Both prompted a retreat from economic reform and, in time, limited the significance of the *Model Proposals* primarily to the realm of economic theorising.

A NEW SYSTEM OF INCENTIVES AND DIRECTIVES

The means of activating enterprises and assessing their performance were of fundamental importance in the new system of economic management. These issues were at the centre of the Economic Council's debates and Kalecki's ideas strongly influenced the Council's recommendations.

The setting up of a new price structure had to be the starting point in arranging a new system of incentives and directives for key industrial enterprises – planning and management in less important enterprises were to be thoroughly decentralised. The new prices were to be ensure the proper functioning of incentives (see pp. 49–54 below). In addition to this system of factory prices, Kalecki proposed a system of enterprise management consisting of four interacting elements:

(1) *Net output*, as the basic indicator of planned activity in the enterprise;
(2) a *wage fund limit*, determined mainly by the net output indicator;
(3) the increase in profits relative to the previous period, forming the basis for bonus payments to the workforce;
(4) interest to be paid on non-returnable investment credits.

As was mentioned above, the net output indicator was supposed to link the operations of the enterprise with the central plan. This indicator, which was set for the enterprise by its supervisory agency, was a directive target. Its fulfilment or overfulfilment was not, however, linked to any financial benefits for the enterprise. Meeting this target was to be the managerial responsibility of the enterprise director, who would be entitled to demand co-operation from the workers' council in fulfilling this task. As we shall see later, other incentives proposed by Kalecki were to encourage the enterprise to fulfil and overfulfil the net output target.

Kalecki suggested that net output should be calculated as the difference between the value of total output, expressed in constant factory (that is, exclusive of turnover or sales tax) prices, and the value of materials, fuel and semi-fabricates, also in constant prices. This gave the net output indicator a more synthetic character: the enterprise could increase its net output not just by increasing total production, but also by materials-saving.

The wage bill limit was calculated on the basis of the previous year's limit, increased in proportion to the increase in net output. As a rule, this allowed for earnings to increase faster than would be warranted by an increase in employment or piece-work payments. The excess was to be ear-marked for various kinds of bonus payments, for example, to the technical and managerial staff, or for materials-savings. In this way, the wages fund limit would act as an incentive to increase net output with a given level of employment.

However, this method of setting the wage fund limit would not inspire any increases in overall net output, but only in net output per worker. In order to achieve this the wages fund limit was supplemented by enterprise profit-sharing. This share would depend not on the level of profits, but would be a percentage of the increase in profits. The base level of profits in this calculation would be adjusted for the effects of factors independent of the economic performance of the enterprise which would have deprived this incentive of its objective character. Furthermore, in order to make profit-related bonuses independent of unpredictable fluctuations in production (due to irregular deliveries of raw materials and so on) Kalecki proposed that the basis of these bonuses should be, say, a three-year moving average of adjusted profits.

Finally, in Kalecki's opinion, profit should only be calculated on production sold. This would encourage the production of marketable output, an incentive which the wage fund limit, based on net output, could not furnish.

The effectiveness of the incentives contained in the wage fund limit and enterprise profit-sharing depended on the way in which factory prices were set. Kalecki proposed a cost-plus formula. But with such a formula, differences in the percentage margin over costs for different products could give rise to undesireable changes in the product mix. Furthermore, the size of the profit margin determined the relative weight in profit increases of cost reductions as opposed to production increases. Kalecki therefore argued that the profit margin should be as far as possible kept the same for the output of a given industry, to avoid these changes in the product mix, and the running down of production of less profitable articles. However, the margin ought to be differentiated according to industry, being higher in those industries where increased production was more important than cost reduction.

In the area of investment, Kalecki suggested that the hitherto centralised investments should be financed from non-repayable interest-bearing credits. A portion of depreciation would be kept by the enterprise; the rest would be paid into a central fund. In exchange for the latter, the enterprise would receive the same rate of interest as would be payable for non-repayable centralised investment credits. Thus the interest earned on the portion of depreciation paid by the state would reduce the burden of interest paid on investment credits. Depreciation funds kept by the enterprise in the bank and not spent would also earn interest at the same rate.

Decentralised investments would be financed by non-repayable credits as well, but at a higher interest rate. This would be the equilibrium rate of interest at which the demand for such credits equalled the sums allocated for them. Kalecki proposed that, in this case, depreciation should be organised on the same principles as for centralised investments. Thus Kalecki wanted the interest rate to play the following role:

> If an economic effect is obtained without additional investment, then the whole benefit of it will accrue to the enterprise, since it does not have to pay any additional interest, while the interest on the capital used is already included in the price. If the effect is the result of new investment, then the enterprise must pay additional interest. This creates an incentive to achieve economic effects without new investments. If the enterprise carries out decentralised investments, then it will pay a higher rate of interest, in return for having undertaken uncontrolled investment. Of course, the enterprise will not pay interest for investments paid for from its own funds.[11]

Thus, in the system of incentives and directives proposed by Kalecki, the enterprise's performance was to be assessed according to its net output and the growth of net output, as well as the additional depreciation and interest paid for credit-financed investments. This system creates incentives to expand net production at the cost of the smallest possible investment, and to reduce material costs. The principles governing the wage fund would provide incentives to increase labour productivity, since any reduction in the workforce, at a constant level of net output, would immediately increase the mean amount of the wage fund per worker. The planned net output indicator would link up the above system of incentives and tie it to the fulfilment of the central plan.

The scheme Kalecki proposed concerned the incentives applied and directives transmitted to the enterprise by the agency in charge of it. If enterprises were grouped into multi-enterprise firms which would be trading companies in their own right, then the supervising agencies would simply become large enterprises. He considered that the incentives and directives issued by the central authorities would then be applied to the whole firm and its net output, wage fund limit, and the profit-sharing payments to the workforce, based on increases in the firm's profits. The incentives and directives set by the management of the firm for its subordinate enterprises could remain the same. But particular firms could if necessary work out their own systems of incentives better adapted to the specific conditions in their industry.[12]

Kalecki's proposals were the subject of lively discussion in various phases of their development, in the Planning Sub-commission of the Economic Council. The dangers were pointed out of creating a special system of accounting for incentives, which would tend to insulate them from actual operating conditions.[13] These issues were also discussed by the Economic Model Commission, in connection with the final draft of the Proposals on the System of Economic Incentives and Economic Calculation, which were presented to the Economic Council on 27 July 1957. In the discussion on these proposals, Kalecki stated that:

> All these proposals are grounded in central planning, and there is no suggestion that enterprises should themselves set prices. Similarly, when it comes to workers' profit-sharing, this is based on changes in profits, and therefore is very far indeed from the Yugoslav system. Here all incentives are subordinate to the fulfilment or over-fulfilment of the plan.
>
> In only one respect do these proposals depart from the present system. This is in not making all bonsues and other payments dependent upon plan fulfilment, which leads to reductions in the plan and is exactly what has been rejected. In fact this is the classical system of central planning, amended so that bonuses are not paid for plan fulfilment.[14]

In fact, the discussion at the Fifth Plenary Meeting of the Economic Council ended the theoretical disputes on the new system of economic incentives. The proposals agreed then were in many respects similar to those put forward by Kalecki.[15] As in the case of the *Model Proposals*, the greatest difficulties arose not in reaching a compromise agreement in the Economic Council, but in implementing the incentives proposals in practice.

HORIZONTAL ASSOCIATIONS OR VERTICAL FIRMS

The discussion about the new economic model demonstrated the importance of the relationship between an autonomous enterprise and its supervising agency which was supposed to replace the central boards of enterprises. Kalecki rejected the suggestion that central boards should simply be replaced by associations of enterprises, because it introduced no new element and merely transferred the principle of enterprise autonomy on to a higher intermediary. From the very start of the Economic Council's activities, he put forward the alternative idea of creating vertically integrated supervisory units; that is, vertically integrated firms. He visualised the organisational structure of the supervisory agency as follows:

> There is one man responsible for management, a director nominated by the authorities, apart from whom there exists a council which decides on general policy. But there is a difference in the supervisory agency in comparison with the enterprise. In the former, the members of the council would not just include representatives of enterprises' councils, but also management representatives and, where necessary, representatives nominated by the ministry or the government. It seems to me that this would simply weaken the structure of the council and the role of enterprise directors in the supervising agency . . . It may or may not be a vertical concern, but it ought to account for itself economically and should not be responsible for the output of a whole industry. The latter is even more important than how many enterprise representatives there should be on the firm's council.[16]

However, the organisational structure for the supervisory agencies proposed by the Party Central Committee's Commission on Workers' Councils and Management, in the second half of 1957, favoured horizontal integration. Kalecki could do little but acknowledge the flexibility of the proposed solution. This envisaged the creation of conglomerate enterprises where this did not present difficulties, as well as the grouping together as far as possible of enterprises whose production was complementary. He saw one of the most important tasks of the new associations as being the setting of such contract prices as would best reflect conditions of production in each enterprise.

The weakness of this scheme was its ambiguity as to which material incentives were to secure the proper operation of the enterprise associations. This was a fundamental problem. If its staff was paid out of the profits of the association as a whole, then this might encourage the board to set contract prices in such a way as to secure the highest profits. Moreover, these incentives should also take account of the economic results of all the associated enterprises.

Somewhat earlier, Kalecki had put forward a scheme to resolve this problem, according to which enterprises within vertically or horizontally integrated firms would retain a higher degree of autonomy. For its part, the central economic administration was not to intervene in the internal affairs of the concern, but only to supply it with its essential inputs and take into account the final economic results of the firm as a whole. The firm's board would direct its enterprises by a system of directives and incentives adapted to the specific conditions in which the enterprises operated. But all incentives and directives applied by the authority in charge of the firm would be based on the firm's aggregate results – that is, its aggregate marketed output, profits and so on as a whole. The funds which the concern would receive for bonuses, general and above plan profit-sharing, and so on, would finance material incentives for the individual enterprises as well as for the management of the firm.

> Thus there would be strong financial links between the firm as a whole and the individual enterprises that make it up. The better the firm co-ordinates its constituent enterprises the better overall results it will achieve, and the greater the funds that it will have at its disposal to distribute to its enterprises in the form of bonuses, shares in profits, etc. But the firm's overall results would obviously depend on the achievements of the individual enterprises.[17]

Kalecki felt that the firm should be managed like an individual enterprise and have its own workers' self-management. Although the notion of any industry-wide integration of workers' councils was severely criticised by Gomułka as early as May 1957 (see above, pp. 32–3), Kalecki continued to support such a development.

> It seems to me to be necessary that not only enterprise directors but also the workers' councils should be represented in enterprise associations, since the councils are not nominated by any supervisory authority. I consider this to be of fundamental significance for the way in which enterprises operate. If an enterprise has a decision imposed on it without the participation of its workers' council, then this can cause friction . . . If the workers' council participates in decision-making, then there will be co-operation in the process of price-setting.[18]

Kalecki also pointed out that with uniform supply prices for the enterprise association, and differentiated accounting prices for its enterprises, the resulting profit should be so distributed among enterprises as to encourage them to reduce costs. The staff of the association should have a financial interest in its profits overall. This would encourage the association to allocate production among its enterprises with due regard for economic efficiency. In this way the association would become a profit-maximiser with respect to its enterprises as a whole. In Kalecki's opinion, this question required detailed investigation. Above all, it required an appropriate system of accounting prices which would encourage cost-reduction in enterprises, and induce associations to allocate production efficiently so as to obtain the highest joint profit.[19]

A resolution of the Council of Ministers on 18 April 1958 created enterprise associations in place of the existing central boards in key industry. It also allowed vertical concentration in those industries where conditions for this existed. The resolution emphasised the structural flexibility of these supervisory authorities. However, the associations rapidly took over from the central boards the tradition of administrative management of enterprises and did not manifest any desire to make use of their rights to adapt management to the specific conditions in particular industries. The hope that ministries would restrain the monopolistic tendencies of the association also went unfulfilled.

As for the notion of vertically-integrated firms advocated at the time by Kalecki, its difficulties arose mainly from its dependence on the general strategy of economic development, a dependence that was by no means clearly understood at the time. Where a certain degree of vertical integration was natural, for example in the metallurgical, chemical and textiles industries, such firms had already been set up earlier. The main task was therefore to set them up in other industries, primarily in the machine-building industry. Here, however, vertical integration makes sense only in large-scale production, far exceeding that required to supply the markets of one or even a few medium-sized economies. An essential precondition therefore was that some fundamental decisions about selective economic development and directions for international specialisation in production needed to be taken. Kalecki was aware of these prior conditions and he made efforts in the Polish Planning Commission and in the Economic Commission of the Council for Mutual Economic Assistance aimed at co-ordinating the principles for division of labour and specialisation among the member countries of the

CMEA. This would have created the opportunity for vertically integrated firms to function economically. However, these attempts brought results that were far below his expectations.

PRICES

In the discussions between 1954 and 1956 the system of prices had already been sharply criticised, and the need to set factory prices that would enable enterprises to operate rational economic calculation had been argued. The price reform of 1 January 1956 was intended to eliminate the differences between factory prices and the costs of production for investment goods, and thereby to reduce subsidies to those factories which manufactured these goods. However, the reform only partially fulfilled the hopes placed in it, and the need for changes in the price system remained urgent.

From 1956 a handful of selected factories was granted more autonomy in a limited programme of economic experiments. Workers in these factories almost without exception started demanding increases in the supply prices of their output. While the Economic Council's Sub-Commission on Experiments was left to face these pressures, the work of the Prices Sub-Commission concentrated on the general principles of constructing a new system of prices. This was primarily to reflect the social costs of production, equate supply and demand in markets, act as incentives to enterprises, and serve the central planner as a parameter in long-term economic decision-making, to mention only a few basic functions.

The only indisputable proposition at that stage was that the starting point of any price system had to be a proper calculation of raw material costs. Together with Stanisław Polaczek, Kalecki attempted to resolve this problem. They proposed that the domestic relative prices of raw materials which are, or could be, traded abroad should correspond to their relative prices in foreign trade. In this way the financial effects of using or saving these raw materials in domestic production, calculated in domestic currency, would not differ from the balance of payments effects. The inconsistency between the interests of enterprises, expressed in terms of złotys, and the interests of the economy as a whole, expressed in terms of foreign currency, could thus be removed.

Kalecki and Polaczek argued that the domestic prices of raw materials should be set on the basis of an appropriate exchange rate.[20] This was not to exceed a 'ceiling rate'; that is, the rate at which, at a given level of retail prices and money wages, and a given level of employment, export revenue covered costs. Setting a rate higher that the 'ceiling rate' would pose the danger of a balance of payments deficit. Industrial and agricultural raw materials' prices were set in a similar way, within the parameters set by the desired distribution of income between urban and rural areas. This was only one of a number of conditions to be satisfied by the exchange rate for raw materials.

The Kalecki and Polaczek proposals were discussed in the Planning Commission and the Economic Council. The Prices Sub-Commission of the Economic Council largely incorporated them into its 'Tezy w sprawie cen podstawowych surowców' ('Proposals on Raw Materials Prices').[21] The main points of this document were in turn included in the draft 'Tezy Rady Ekonomicznej w sprawie zasad kształtowania cen' ('Economic Council Proposals on the Principles of Price Determination').

Once the principles of determining prices for raw materials were agreed, the discussions on the Economic Council's draft concentrated on how factory prices should be set. Kalecki and many others came out decidedly in favour of a cost-plus pricing formula, and against prices derived from markets.[22] The fundamental difficulties arose, however, out of the question of what costs of production were to form the basis of factory prices. Were these to be average or marginal costs? Tied up with this issue was, of course, the matter of incentives.

The starting point for Kalecki's factory price formula was the cost of raw materials inputs, calculated in line with the above-mentioned principles of raw materials' pricing. To the raw materials' cost was to be added labour costs, depreciation, and then a margin consisting of two elements: a percentage mark up on fixed capital, and on labour cost. At higher stages of production the cost of semi-fabricates would replace that of raw materials.

The next problem which arises under the cost of production, as opposed to the market-derived, system of price determination is that of the relationship between (short-run) equilibrium prices and the costs of production. If the market equilibrium price exceeded the cost of production in a particular enterprise, Kalecki proposed that the difference should be taxed away by a turnover tax. Furthermore, assuming that subsidies would not be paid to enterprises whose cost of production was higher than their market price, then the market mechanism would indicate in which enterprises production was economically viable, and in which it was not. This would be consistent with textbook models of free competition, except that enterprises with lower costs of production would not enjoy a differential rent. However, if no subsidies are paid and if, as in Kalecki's scheme, no real market mechanism operates, then the question of how to decide which factories should operate and which should not is left open.

In the case of investment goods, one can say that the demand for them can be derived from the output plan, since as many of them will have to be produced as is necessary to meet the output targets throughout the economy. But even here many problems occur. A still more difficult situation arises in the case of consumer goods, for which no similiar demand schedule can be drawn up. The equilibrium price, unless it is determined by the market mechanism, depends on how many plants produce a given product and in what quantities. Kalecki proposed therefore that the 'price of production' should be based on the average cost of production when all plants in an industry operated on given supplies of raw materials.[23]

If the market equilibrium price is less than the price of production, there arises the additional problem of whether to subsidise more costly production, or whether to reduce output by shutting down the high cost producers. Kalecki regarded this as an important and open political question:

> If we shut down an enterprise and the workers formerly employed there are out of work, then . . . overall national income is reduced. It can be said that this will save imported raw materials, and that . . . one can import other, more useful raw materials instead. . . . However, then we have unemployed workers and the obligation to support them in the same standard of living as they previously enjoyed . . . In capitalist enterprises, this is simple, since a shutdown implies losses for the capitalist who, however, feels no responsibility for his workers. But the socialist state does have that responsibility. Therefore, thinking aloud, to apply this system and shut down in all such cases cannot be done; neither can subsidies be paid in all instances.[24]

The Economic Council's Proposals on Price Determination mentioned above were an attempt at a compromise that ultimately proved impossible to achieve. At the sixth plenary meeting of the Council in November 1957, the proposals failed to obtain the approval of the majority of Council members. Further public discussion of them dealt essentially with only two issues:

(1) the 'standard pricing formula' which ought to become the basis for price setting; and
(2) the principles proposed by Kalecki and Polaczek for determining the prices of raw materials.

Some of the critical comments on the proposals did not elicit any polemics despite the undoubtedly debatable objections that were raised.[25] However, as a radical reform of the economy, aimed at granting genuine autonomy to enterprises and their workforce, was abandoned, these discussions became increasingly more academic.

It is interesting to note that in the course of Economic Council's debates on the function of prices in the allocation of resources in a socialist economy Kalecki took a line which was little different to that taken by him ten years earlier. In the autumn of 1947, in a discussion on a paper by Oskar Lange, 'Praktyka planowania gospodarczego a optymalna alokacja zasobów' ('The Practice of Planning and the Optimum Allocation of Resources'), Kalecki pointed out that it was a fundamental mistake to compare a real economic system with one that had never existed. He said:

> The present planned or controlled economies are being compared to the capitalist economy as it was pictured in textbooks until recent times, where it was endowed with perfect equalisation of marginal cost and prices, negligible unemployment, optimum distribution of resources, and so on and so forth. In fact, it was an apologistic myth of the capitalist economy and nothing of the sort has ever existed. Prices were never equal to marginal cost; unemployment was considerable, and so on. It is from this point of view that the problems of the present discussion should be considered.
>
> . . . In considering the planned and controlled economies of devastated countries, you have to compare them with what would actually have happened if their economies were 'free'. An extreme shift to profits from other incomes would take place under present circumstances and the demand for luxury goods would influence to a great extent the pattern of production. Now, however great are the difficulties of planning production in Eastern Europe, I

still prefer the priorities established by it to those determined by the demand of black marketeers.[26]

Kalecki's approach to price determination in a socialist economy was partly influenced by his experience of oligopoly pricing practices in capitalist economies, and his awareness of the highly monopolised structure of Polish industry. For these reasons among others, he emphasised the need for permanent price controls. Generally speaking, his idea of socialist pricing policy was not prices set by 'unrestrained market' forces, but 'correct' (perhaps even 'just') prices.

Rigid prices set by competing duopolies and oligopolies by means of tacit and overt price agreements, and the multiplier effects of investment, Kalecki regarded as essential features of oligopolist capitalism. In contrast to this, he saw the socialist economy with centralised price determination as characterised by flexible prices, which the central planner could always adjust to a level corresponding to full capacity operation and a given share of investments in national income, with the multiplier effects absent from the system.

Kalecki regarded a socialist economy in which enterprises set prices as something extraordinary. He warned that phenomena similar to those appearing in oligopoly capitalism might emerge in such circumstances. Socialist enterprises could enter into agreements to maintain rigid prices. Imperfect competition, typical under concentrated production, might also emerge. At the same time, the undesirable consequences of the multiplier effect might appear too. Finally, Kalecki pointed out that in such a system unjustifiable income differentiation among workers employed in different enterprises could come into being, and this could not be a matter of indifference from the point of view of socialist social relations.[27] In his subsequent studies on the socialist economy, Kalecki never abandoned the principle of centralised price determination for all products, with the exception of locally produced goods satisfying local needs.

It is worth pointing out in this context that price-setting mechanisms remain at the centre of economic reform debates in Poland, Hungary, the Soviet Union, and other CMEA countries. The resolution of this issue predetermines the scope for a genuine market mechanism envisaged under respective reform proposals. Kalecki's restrained approach implies, in practice, not money but rather quasi-money relations in the socialist economy. Nevertheless, it continues to attract support in these debates, partly because the dangers of monopolistic pricing practices (on the part of large as well as small producers) are only too real in those countries.

Notes

1. See transcript of the meeting of the Economic Model Commission of the Economic Council, held on 4 March 1957 (Archives of the Council of Ministers – henceforth AURM – ref. 545/2). See also M. Kalecki, *Dzieła*, vol. III, p. 336.
2. M. Kalecki, 'Nie przeceniać roli modelu' ('Do not overestimate the importance of the Model'), in *Dzieła*, vol. III, p. 108.
3. M. Kalecki, *Dzieła*, vol III, p. 340. See also the transcript of the meeting in the Council of Ministers Archives, AURM ref. 545/13/3.
4. See transcript of the meeting of the Economic Model Commission, AUPM 545/13/14. See also M. Kalecki, *Dzieła*, vol. III, p. 343.
5. The full text of the *Model Proposals* was published in *Życie Gospodarcze*, 1957, no. 22, and they were extensively discussed in the daily press at the beginning of June 1957.
6. See minute no. 55 of the Meeting of the Board of the Planning Commission on 6 July 1957, Planning Commission Archives (henceforth AKPRM) ref. 5/78. Kalecki, who was a member of that Board did not attend this meeting.
7. M. Kalecki, *Dzieła*, vol. III, pp. 348–9.
8. *Życie Gospodarcze* (1957), no. 24 and C. Bobrowski, *Wspomnienia ze stulecia*, (*Recollections from the Century*) (Lublin: Wydawnictwo Lubelskie, 1985), pp. 245–6.
9. Even more important was the termination of forced collectivisation in agriculture announced by Gomułka on his return to power, and his approval for private farming. Since this change occurred outside the scope of Kalecki's activities, we shall not deal with it here.
10. See C. Bobrowski, *Wspomnienia ze stulecia*, pp. 249–50.
11. M. Kalecki, *Dzieła*, vol. III, p. 114.
12. M. Kalecki, 'Outline of a New System of Incentives and Directives', in *Selected Essays on Economic Planning*.
13. See, for example, the papers by W. Brus and M. Kuczyński presented to the Planning Sub-Commission in June 1957, AURM 545/13/18.
14. M. Kalecki, *Dzieła*, vol. III, p. 366. See also the transcript of the fifth plenary meeting of the Economic Council, AURM 545/13/418.
15. The Council's proposals were discussed and elucidated in M. Kalecki, 'Outline of a new system . . .'
16. M. Kalecki, *Dzieła*, vol. III, p. 357. See also the transcript of the third plenary meeting of the Economic Council, AURM 545/13/3.
17. M. Kalecki, 'The Vertically-Integrated Firm as an Element in the New Economic Model', in *Selected Essays on Economic Planning*.
18. M. Kalecki, *Dzieła*, vol. III, p. 359. See also the transcript of the Economic Model Commission meeting held on 17 January 1958, AURM 545/

27/16. According to information given to the author by Włodzimierz Brus, during discussions at the Economic Council of the *Model Proposals*, the majority of the participants came out in favour of workers' council representation on the boards of industrial associations. However, the full-time deputy chairman, Czesław Bobrowski, was aware that inclusion of this demand in the text of the Proposals would be a stumbling block for the authorities. He therefore suggested that no formal resolution about the matter be voted on, but that an appropriate statement be included in a footnote. In the version published by *Życie Gospodarcze* this footnote was actually published, but in the book version which came out shortly afterwards, it was deleted.

19. See the minutes of the eighth plenary meeting of the Economic Council on 13 February 1958, AURM 545/13/9, p. 6.
20. Minutes of the Planning Commission meeting held on 19 March 1957, AKPRM 5/81; and M. Kalecki and S. Polaczek, 'Uwagi w sprawie ustalenia cen surowców podstawowych'. ('Notes on the Setting of Prices for Raw Materials'), in M. Kalecki, *Dzieła*, vol. III, pp. 131–40. Initially, the accounting exchange rate for raw materials was estimated on the basis of the ratio of retail prices of wage goods, excluding the retailers' margin, to the value of these articles expressed in foreign currency. (The retail prices used were those which would be introduced as a result of the changes in raw materials' prices in 1956.)
21. Prices Sub-Commission, Economic Council, AURM 546/23/23.
22. M. Kalecki, *Dzieła*, vol. III, pp. 378–9, and the transcript of the fifth plenary meeting of the Economic Council, held on 27 July 1957, AURM 545/13/18.
23. AURM 545/13/18.
24. M. Kalecki, *Dzieła*, vol. III, p. 381.
25. The course of the discussion was partly influenced by the fact that no comprehensive commentary on the 'Price Proposals' had appeared earlier. Włodzimierz Brus' article 'Niektóre problemy teorii cen w gospodarce socjalistycznej' ('Some Problems of Price Theory in the Socialist Economy'), which could have fulfilled this role, appeared only in 1958, in O. Lange (ed.), *Zagadnienia ekonomii politycznej socjalizmu* (*Problems in the Political Economy of Socialism*) (Warsaw: Książka i Wiedza) when the debates were already quite advanced.
26. M. Kalecki, 'Contributions to the Discussion on the paper of Oskar Lange', *Proceedings of the International Statistical Conference*, Washington D.C., 6–18 September 1947, The Econometric Society Meeting, vol. V, pp. 176–7.
27. M. Kalecki, 'Central Price Determination as an Essential Feature of a Socialist Economy', in *Selected Essays on Economic Planning*.

4 Long-Term Planning

THE PRELIMINARY METHODOLOGICAL ASSUMPTIONS OF KALECKI'S PERSPECTIVE PLANNING

In the middle of 1956, a working party was set up in the Planning Commission, on the initiative of its then chairman, Eugeniusz Szyr, to work on perspective plans. On 29 July 1957, the Council of Ministers adopted a resolution authorising work on a perspective plan for Polish economic development from 1961 to 1975. Two months later, on 28 September, the new Chairman of the Planning Commission, Stefan Jędrychowski, appointed a Perspective Plan Commission (Komisja Główna Planu Perspektywicznego), under the chairmanship of Michał Kalecki. The research and administrative functions for the Commission were carried out by a specially organised Perspective Plan Office (*Zakład Planów Perspektywicznych*).

Kalecki's idea of perspective planning was the setting up of a kind of planning infrastructure covering the economy as a whole, as well as particular industries, large industrial plants and regions. Such planning was to form a basis for a broad debate which was to result in the drawing up of various alternative development strategies and options for future economic development. The work on the perspective plan required different needs, including local and industrial ones, to be taken into account and analysed. The economic effectiveness of alternative ways of meeting those needs were then compared. Finally, and particularly important, was the assessment of these alternative development strategies in the light of their micro-economic efficiency in satisfying overall economic needs.

The main task of the perspective plan was not to show how Poland would look in 1975, although obviously it would have been useful to obtain such a picture. However, there were too many imponderable factors (technological progress, foreign trade, and so on) for any such picture to be sufficiently accurate. The perspective plan was not meant to be a directive plan. Its aim was only to define the directions of future development. As such, it was supposed to be revised in the successive phases of its preparation. The essence of perspective planning and its main purpose was to set guidelines, primarily for the drawing up of five year plans, but also for annual ones. Hence the necessity for these studies and research to be permanent and continuous.

This was a departure from the accepted theory and practice in the Planning Commission in at least two respects. First of all, the Perspective Plan Office worked not so much through the industrial departments of the Planning Commission, as through its own specialists operating in those departments. Secondly, the Office rejected the principle of formulating the plan on the basis of questionnaires returned by individual industrial departments. The argument was that every questionnaire limits the scope of the information that it can obtain to that defined by the questions it contains. The Office wanted to identify much broader interdependencies than those which could be captured in any questionnaire. Therefore the questionnaire was replaced by a short analysis outlining the concept of perspective planning.

This analysis, *Wstępne tezy ogólnych założeń planu perspektywicznego na lata 1961–1975 (Preliminary General Assumptions for the 1961–1975 Perspective Plan)*[1] was prepared under Kalecki's supervision in 1957. It was the basis for the whole enterprise. These '*Preliminary Assumptions*' put forward hypotheses about economic and social development in the perspective plan period, worked out a methodology for long-term planning, and set out the probable order of magnitude of basic constituents of the plan in 1975. Thus, a skeleton plan and the main directions of development were outlined.

The methodology of the analysis rested on the following assumptions:

(1) The share of productive investment in national income determines the rate of economic growth. However, in estimating national income, a different method of accounting was used from that hitherto used in Poland. In calculating national income produced at supply prices, three adjustments were made. Firstly turnover tax was deducted from the value of industrial output. Secondly, the balance of price differences between the relative internal and external prices of imports and exports was eliminated. Thirdly, the difference between the imputed agricultural incomes valued at retail prices minus the trading margin and its value in constant 1956 agricultural prices was taken out.

(2) On the basis of the assumed growth of rural and urban housebuilding, a growth rate of non-productive investment was projected.

(3) Consumption expenditure was calculated as the difference between the gross national income distributed at wholesale prices (obtained by adding back to gross national income produced the deductions made in calculating national income produced under the procedure described in (1) above), and the gross accumulation fund (including non-productive accumulation).
(4) Demographic assumptions were supplied by the central statistical service GUS (Główny Urząd Statystyczny). On this basis, population forecasts were worked out, together with comparative labour supply projections.
(5) An analysis of food consumption was carried out using (a) physiological norms of consumption, and (b) comparative analyses of the consumption of specific articles in countries with high standards of living. The increase in the consumption of industrial articles was calculated by deducting from the consumption fund the value of food consumption. The increase in the value of clothing consumption (assuming a rate of growth for this equal to that of consumption overall) was then deducted to obtain the growth of consumer durables demand.
(6) Employment in large and medium-sized industry was estimated by extrapolating over 1961–75 the growth rate of employment obtained from the ratio of the increase in labour supply to that of plant and machinery in the five-year plan for 1956–60. The growth of employment in small-scale industry and construction was estimated on the basis of assumptions about labour productivity growth. Employment growth in services was reckoned as a function of planned improvements in services. In this way it was possible to check the feasibility of the initial projections of national income and investment growth rates against labour supply projections.
(7) Using material balances, an estimate of import requirements was made. This then gave a preliminary estimate of the necessary export growth.
(8) Estimates of industrial production and demand for it, broken down by industry, were made as follows:
    (a) For the food industry, estimates were based on preliminary assumptions about consumption and export potential.
    (b) For other consumer articles, estimates were based on assumptions about the growth of consumer demand.
    (c) In the machine industry, projections were based on assumptions about investment and foreign trade.

(d) In the building materials industry, projections were based on assumptions about housing construction (broken down into rural and urban housing) and other planned investment.
(e) For the metallurgical industry, estimates were based on projected rolled steel requirements and export potential.
(f) Coal industry estimates were based on assumption of a maximum rate of future extraction, in turn drawn up using preliminary coal market projections.
(g) Electricity supply estimates were made using future household and industrial demand estimates.
(h) For the chemicals industry, projections were based on the rate of growth of this industry in developed countries.

(9) The targets for agricultural development were set on the basis of food demand and anticipated increased yields in the future.[2]

Kalecki's article 'Kilka uwag o planie perspektywicznym 1961–1975[3] ('Some Observations on the 1961–1975 Perspective Plan') which appeared at the beginning of February 1958, was a kind of progress report on the first phase of work on the perspective plan, and the problems arising during it. Kalecki included among the main tasks of the plan:

(1) raising standards of living as much as possible and especially achieving the food consumption norms laid down by physiologists;
(2) reaching reasonable standards of housing by 1975;
(3) the maintenance of full employment;
(4) plan realism, and not having to rely on potential loans from abroad.

Kalecki also pointed to the main bottleneckes in economic development over this period, namely the limited potential for expanding hard coal production, and the problems in balancing foreign trade. But he considered it feasible to achieve in Poland, in the final year of the plan, the standard of living in 1960 of the wealthier European countries. However, this required immediate, strenuous and co-ordinated organisational and other efforts in all sectors of the economy. He also emphasised that another necessary condition for the achievement of the aims of the plan was the speedy co-ordination of perspective plans in the member countries of the CMEA, resulting in specialisation and the consequent long-term trade agreements between them.

FROM PRELIMINARY GENERAL ASSUMPTIONS TO DETAILED PROVISIONS

The 'Założenia do szczegółowych prac nad planem perspektywicznym 1961–1975'[4] ('Detailed Working Assumptions for the 1961–1975 Perspective Plan'), were a further developed and improved version of the 'Preliminary General Assumptions'. One of the most difficult problems here was the question of integrating micro-economic issues with the macro-economic analysis and especially how to integrate national income with fixed capital and changes in it. Kalecki, who was himself one of the pioneers of econometrics, was fairly sceptical about econometric methods. He considered that an econometric approach could not itself create a conceptual framework if this had not been defined first. The economist must have his own appreciation of the meaning of particular indicators and the limits of their applications. He or she must not only know how particular indicators are related to each other, but must also be aware of the inferences that can, and those that cannot, be drawn from them, which are direct and which are derivative or have a high probability of error. As a result, the relationship between the growth of national income and that of fixed capital that was followed in the 'Preliminary General Assumptions' and in the 'Detailed Working Assumptions' did not rely on an econometric approach but on the methodology put forward by Kalecki in 'Dynamika inwestycji i dochodu narodowego w gospodarce socjalistycznej' ('The Growth of Investment and National Income in the Socialist Economy').[5]

Kalecki also pointed out that such aggregate concepts as the value of fixed capital or total depreciation in the economy as a whole have such high margins of error that drawing conclusions from relationships based on them could lead to serious mistakes undermining the whole project. In analysing the factors contributing to economic growth, he avoided using concepts derived from the value of fixed capital and depreciation. He thought that the risk of error was significantly reduced if the rate of economic growth is related to investment instead.

In this phase of the project there were many other such issues. For example, Kalecki considered that consumption and related categories of expenditure ought to be related to the prices at which they are ultimately sold. But these prices could not be used in determining output growth since the distortions in them might lead to absurd results.[6] For this reason, in the perspective plan, production targets were expressed in factory prices (that is, in prices which did not include turnover tax). Hence also the concept of national income in which consumption was related to final sales prices, and accumulation to factory prices.

This work contributed to the development of comparative studies of national income and its structure in Poland and other CMEA countries. Kalecki himself made numerous efforts to apply the new concept of national income and material product balances in the other CMEA countries (see below, pp. 76–7). This analysis also gave rise to the first empirical study of input–output flows. Estimates of material costs, on which output analysis is based, were necessary for the perspective plan. But since the structure of material costs was estimated, using 1957 production and consumption flows in value terms, further work that was already being done by the Central Statistical Office led to the drawing up, in 1957–62, of a number of experimental input–output models, and subsequently to the *Bilans przepływów międzygałęziowych w gospodarce narodowej Polski – 1962* (*An Input–Output Model of the Polish Economy in 1962*).[7]

At the end of May 1958, the Perspective Plan Office sent out its 'Detailed Assumptions' to all parties concerned. They were discussed that year at the eleventh plenary meeting of the Economic Council, on 19 July, in the Board of the Planning Commission on 29 September, in the Institute of Economics of the Polish Academy of Sciences on 15 November, and at a meeting of the Prime Minister's Advisory Council on Technology.

In the Planning Commission the discussion concentrated on the problem of relating the goals of the perspective plan to those of the 1961–5 Five Year Plan. The discussions at the Economic Council and in the Economic Institute of the Polish Academy of Sciences were more fundamental. They were based on Kalecki's widely known papers in which he outlined the aims and methodology of perspective planning, and the essential elements of what he believed was a feasible plan.[8]

In the course of these discussions, Kalecki emphasised that the perspective plan was not intended to be a comprehensive presentation of the whole process of economic development from 1961 to 1975. The plan was supposed to be continually modified in the light of the latest forecasts of development in order to arrive at informed solutions to the economic problems of the time. Already longer-term forecasts had been necessary in drawing up the 1961–5 Five Year

Plan. From this point of view, the perspective plan had been something of a success, since it made that task easier by providing the basis for working out that Five-Year Plan. Kalecki supposed that in future the perspective plan would be a moving fifteen-year plan, so that in drawing up the next Five Year Plan (1966–70) a perspective plan moved five years ahead (that is for 1966–80) would be used.

The most heated controversies were aroused by the rate of growth of national income and gross social output. Many participants pointed out that the perspective plan's projected growth rate was lower than that of the 1961–5 Five Year Plan. The authors of the perspective plan were accused of drawing it up in accordance with a bourgeois theory of a 'damped curve' of development. Kalecki categorically rejected this charge. He explained that they had not been guided by any doctrine, of either damped or accelerating growth. If the projected growth rate declined, this was because of the objective economic factors that had been taken into account in the plan.

Why then did the authors of the plan choose this and not another rate of national income growth? Their starting point was the actual rate of growth achieved in the 1956–60 period. But this proved not to be feasible in the longer term because of difficulties in balancing foreign trade, the appearance of bottlenecks in certain industries, and limited markets for newly exported goods. Bottlenecks appeared in particular in coal-mining. The limited possibilities for opening up a large number of new pits, and the average ten-year gestation period for these investments severely constrained the rate of increase of coal production. The projected 30 per cent increase would in any case be very difficult to achieve. In general, because of long construction periods, the high economic growth rates postulated made it necessary to construct a large number of new plants. But if the number of different construction sites in operation at any one time becomes very high this gives rise to difficulties in controlling and managing efficiently such a wide investment front.

A second focus of criticism in the perspective plan, compared to the 1956–60 Five Year Plan, was that the former postulated a lower economic growth rate with approximately the same share of productive investment in national income. But there were many favourable factors improving the effectiveness of productive investment in the 1956–60 period: it reaped the benefits of the heavy investments already started under the auspices of the Six Year Plan in 1950–55, and investment during the subsequent five-year period was intentionally concentrated on completion work in the broad sense. This of course accounted for the high efficiency of investment in the latter period. Spare capacity was also brought into production and this allowed national output to be raised (especially in agriculture) without additional investment. On the other hand, in the first five years of the perspective plan for 1961–75, it was planned to start several large new investment projects precisely because in 1956–60 such investments had not been undertaken. An improvement in the utilisation of existing capacity was planned for 1961–5, but a lesser one thereafter.

In the perspective plan, non-productive investment was planned to rise much more rapidly than national income, while consumption was to rise somewhat more slowly. Kalecki explained this disparity as follows. It is an over-simplification to say that increasing non-productive investment and consumption is the ultimate aim of socialist production. Its true purpose is to increase consumption and services, the basis for which is created by non-productive investment. What is important is not increasing non-productive investment itself, but the stocks which it provides (for example the number of homes). It is this increase which should be compared with the growth of consumption. This comparison reveals that such stocks did not rise as fast as consumption, even though non-productive investment itself rose more quickly. The plan postulated the virtual doubling of per capita merchandise consumption between 1961 and 1975. In services such as housing, this increase was smaller but nevertheless considerable.

In discussion, the assumption of a constant level of agricultural employment (which with a planned increase in output of 50 per cent implied a similar increase in labour productivity) was also questioned. It was argued that even with a moderate expansion of agricultural co-operatives, there would be a reduction in agricultural employment. Moreover, if rural–urban migration continued at a rate higher than the rural demographic growth rate, then the rural population would age excessively and this would depress labour productivity in agriculture. In any case, there could be no doubt that should agricultural co-operatives proliferate rapidly, agricultural employment would be reduced considerably. Thus the problem arose of what assumptions to make regarding the expansion of agricultural producer co-operatives.

The organisation of co-operation within the limits of individual farm ownership, and some expansion of producer co-operatives were already included in the perspective plan variant under discussion.

The setting up of producer co-operatives was supposed to be entirely voluntary. Kalecki therefore argued that instead of raising the production targets of the co-operative sector in agriculture it would be more appropriate to supplement it by another variant. This would postulate a faster rate of collectivisation and hence a faster rate of rural–urban labour migration.

In announcing the preparation of a second version of the perspective plan, Kalecki advised that it would not be based on arbitrary assumptions about higher rates of growth. Apart from postulating greater rural–urban migration, the second variant was to be based on projections concerning, for example, technological progress, foreign trade which, while feasible, were not so probable as to be included in the basic variant. He warned that the second variant should not be expected to improve significantly the rate of economic growth, or increase living standards in comparison with the first variant.[9]

Some of the participants in the discussions came out with more fundamental criticism of the perspective plan's assumptions. In their view, the plan should have postulated a much faster rate of development. One critic argued that Poland was part of a community of socialist states and its rate of development should therefore not lag behind that of the Soviet Union and the other socialist countries. He proposed to obtain the additional supplies of raw materials necessary for a higher growth rate through greater imports from the Soviet Union. Another speaker categorically repudiated the decreasing productivity of investment during the period of the plan.[10]

In his reply to this criticism, Kalecki pointed to the newly-published targets in the Soviet economic plan for 1959–65. These dispelled a number of myths about differences in rates of development among the individual countries of the socialist bloc. For it turned out that the Soviet plan anticipated an increase in industrial production between 1959 and 1965 of 80 per cent. Under the Polish perspective plan, net output, rather than gross output, over this period was due to rise by 75 per cent. There was therefore little difference between the Soviet and the Polish growth rates of production while in the case of national income the difference was even less. In the Soviet plan, national income was to grow at a rate that was approximately 2–5 per cent faster than that planned in Poland. Productive investment in the USSR was to rise only slightly faster than national income, so that there was hardly any rise in the share of investment in national income; nor did the Soviet Union expect any great improvement in the productivity of investment.

In answer to other criticisms, Kalecki said that:

as for 'marginal labour reserves', we should be thinking not only of releasing them, but also of using them sensibly. Let us imagine what would happen if we 'released' 2 million people from the agricultural sector. They are supposed to raise farm buildings, but they already do this on their own farms and for this it is not necessary to mobilise this labour. As for land improvement, it is not labour but drain-pipes which are in short supply. Their production is already strained to the limit under the present plan. Furthermore, pipe-laying itself requires skilled labour. Therefore the 'marginal labour reserves' are left to dig trenches, which in any case is a seasonal occupation, or produce construction materials. However, in Polish conditions only primitive brick-firing using large quantities of coal is feasible, while the production of breeze-blocks is limited by cement supplies.

In the discussion, it was agreed that there exist several development bottlenecks, but at some point these were forgotten and only labour productivity was spoken about. However, when the supply of raw materials is limited, increased labour productivity leads only to shorter working time. The same applies to the effects of releasing labour from agriculture by speeding up collectivisation. It would obviously be desirable to shorten the working week, not just to 40 hours but, say, to 36 hours, but not at any price.

The matter of raw materials is by no means as simple . . . If the Soviet Union does not intend to develop its manufacturing at a considerably faster rate than ours, then this indicates that its natural resources are not unlimited. The raw material reserves of the Soviet Union are enormous but, as we have seen, production is limited not just by these reserves, but by technical and organisational factors as well. The newly discovered natural resources are in general in barely accessible regions of the USSR with harsh climatic conditions. We must beware of too readily assuming that the Soviet Union will push ahead with production beyond the Arctic Circle just so that Poland may have a higher rate of economic development.

Trade is exchange based on mutual advantage and not dependence on raw materials support. The Soviet Union cannot be required to exchange unlimited supplies of its raw materials for machines which it can produce at least as well as Poland does . . .

[It was] argued that if mobilising targets are put into the plan

> we shall thereby accelerate technical progress. I am afraid that setting such high targets will achieve advances in manipulating targets rather than technical advance. It is necessary to specify the actual directions of technical progress rather than talking speciously about the influence of 'anonymous' targets. Technical progress can be introduced either 'from above' or with appropriate economic incentives. Targets should reflect estimates of technical progress but do not induce it themselves . . .
>
> Co-operative farming has one great advantage, which is that it improves the conditions of work in agriculture. Developing an awareness of this among farmers will be the mainspring for the expansion of co-operatives. However, it would be dangerous to project in the plan a definite amount of additional labour supply to be obtained by co-operative development, since it would be hard to assess the pace at which the awareness of the advantages of co-operative farming matures.[11]

Anticipating in some respects future criticisms of the perspective plan, Kalecki emphasised that in discussing target economic growth rates in the plan, these should not be raised solely on the basis of abstract and schematic increases in employment and investment. He argued that the industries in which expansion was to take place should be specified. Technical and organisational bottlenecks should be borne in mind as well as the final uses of the output of some industries, and the limited export markets for the output of others. Taking these factors into account would make the rate of economic growth and many specific issues appear in a totally different light.

THE SECOND PLAN APPROXIMATION

In the autumn of 1958, the Perspective Plan Office started the task of checking the 'Detailed Working Assumptions for the 1961–75 Perspective Plan'. This new phase of work was aimed at a more detailed presentation of the 1961–5 Five Year Plan period and took into account the results of the studies conducted by the various Perspective Plan sub-committees and the issues raised in the debates mentioned above and in press discussions. However, the main task was to make the Plan consistent with the *Wytyczne rozwoju PRL w latach 1959–65 (The Development Policy of the Polish People's Republic in 1959–65)* adopted at the twelfth plenary meeting of the

Central Committee of the PUWP in October 1958,[12] and the resolution under the same title of the Third Congress of the Party.[13]

Neither the Central Committee's nor the Party Congress' resolutions were concerned directly with the Perspective Plan. But, just as in the drawing up of that plan the policy decisions regarding the 1961–5 Five Year Plan were paramount considerations, so now the main subject of these resolutions was the fundamental dimensions of Polish economic development between 1959 and 1965.

The draft plan for 1961–5, prepared on the basis of the 'Detailed Assumptions' was criticised at the Central Committee's plenary meeting. As in the earlier discussions, its projections for industrial production, investment, consumption and overall economic growth were denounced as excessively cautious, and its authors were again accused of professing a theoretical tendency to stagnation. It was emphasised that the postulated economic growth rate, and that of its constituents (especially in some branches of industry), would delay catching up with the advanced capitalist countries. Furthermore, it would increase the disparity between Poland's level of development, and that of the Soviet Union, Czechoslovakia and East Germany. The Chairman of the Economic Committee of the Council of Ministers, Eugeniusz Szyr, argued that it was necessary to increase the growth parameters in the 1959–65 Plan:

> the discussion around the growth rate problem has been burdened by exaggerated and biased criticism of the period between 1949 and 1953. This criticism has created an atmosphere of suspicion and a belief that a faster rate of socialist industrialisation must always mean reduced consumption growth and the rise of glaring and painful imbalances. Our experience of this period greatly inhibits our activists, and distorts the methods and content of discussion, while the one-sided presentation of these issues does not help to create the conviction that a higher rate of growth of production, higher investment, and higher living standards, may be achieved simultaneously.[14]

This view was supported at the Third Party Congress by many delegates who argued for higher investment and growth rates in their regions and industries. This view was reinforced by Władysław Gomułka. In his concluding address, he mentioned two fundamental conditions for the successful implementation of the Plan's economic targets:

> 'first of all the achievement of planned increases in labour productivity. Secondly, the acceptance of a rigorous principle that planned outlays on investment can only be revised upwards'.[15]

On the other hand, the Central Committee and Congress resolutions emphasised the need for balanced economic development and maintaining the realism of even 'mobilising' plan targets. Furthermore, the Congress resolution referring to the 1961–5 Plan did not make any more changes to the main proportions in the version of that plan based on the parameters laid down in the perspective plan and the Central Committee resolution.[16]

Therefore, in drawing up a further revision of the Perspective Plan, Kalecki placed the major emphasis on the question of the Plan's internal consistency. He also argued that the need as well as the opportunities for increased output should be demonstrated in the course of upward revisions of plan indicators. Finally, he stubbornly defended those targets and parameters which, if not implemented under the 1961–5 Five Year Plan, would mean lower consumption and non-productive investment.

Simultaneously in 1958, provincial (*voivodship*) authorities started perspective plans within the framework of the national Plan. By the end of the year, all these authorities had drawn up outlines for the economic development of their regions. These outlines were further elaborated and co-ordinated with national development parameters, and industrial plans and sectoral studies in the first half of 1959.[17] The final outcome of this stage of work was the publication, in 1959, of the *Wytyczne do planu perspektywicznego na lata 1961–75* (*Outline Perspective Plan for 1961–75*). An abridged version was known as the Kalecki Plan.[18] It was the first plan in the history of the Planning Commission that took into account regional and industrial differences as well as local interests in areas where there was a heavy concentration of investment. The *voivodship* planning administrations received information and gave their opinions not just on the locally planned economy, as they had done hitherto, but also on centrally planned economic issues.

The Plan for 1965–75 was presented in two versions. The first of these, which was also the more detailed, was treated as the basic variant. The second, more contingent variant, set more ambitious targets for the recovery of coke from low-sintering iron-smelting coal, natural gas extraction, the pace of agricultural collectivisation, the use of foreign trade balances for additional imports and so on.

Both versions of the *Wytyczne* included provisions for adjustments to the plan in the light of the outcome of the 1961–5 Five Year Plan, technological innovations, the expansion of foreign trade, and intra-CMEA specialisation. It was also intended, in a subsequent version to take into account changes in domestic and foreign trade prices. This was in accordance with Kalecki's original idea that each successive version of the plan was to include new elements and corrections to the basic plan indicators.

In August 1959, the Planning Commission met several times to discuss the details of the Outline Perspective Plan. Kalecki explained and defended the basic dimensions of the Plan and its construction. As before, the arguments centred mainly around the rate of overall economic growth and the growth rates of individual industries. Apart from matters peculiar to the interests of particular industries or regions, the fundamental differences between the critics and Kalecki, together with the group working on the Plan under his direction, boiled down to methodological issues.

Kalecki argued that the starting point in determining the planned volume of any output must be its final use. Following logically from this premise, he questioned why any rate of output expansion was needed in each particular case. Would consumption be expanded thereby, and, if so, was it to be of the output whose production they were trying to increase? Perhaps it was to expand production for export? If so, would sufficiently large markets be found abroad for this enhanced production?

Those who did not share or understand this approach and considered that the volume of production should always be set at the maximum of planned productive capacity responded with mistrust and incomprehension to Kalecki's demands that increased planned output targets should be justified. However, behind his demands lay a fear that the acceleration in production could end up 'in low gear', with economic growth rising from, say, 5 per cent to 10 per cent per annum, but with no increase in consumption or exports, and the higher growth rate therefore reflecting simply higher materials utilisation in production. For this reason, in the first stages of work on the Plan, Kalecki set the lowest possible rates of growth of production that would achieve projected consumption and foreign trade targets. Even if he and his closest colleagues felt this approach to be in some respects inadequate, they feared higher growth 'in lower gear' even more. They regarded their main purpose to be to avoid economic inefficiency in implementing targets for final output.

(Kalecki later generalised the essence of this approach into the first of his basic principles of long-term planning – see pp. 89–90 below.)

In December 1959, Kalecki travelled to India. During his absence, a conference was held of the Planning Commission which was also attended by Vice-Premiers Zenon Nowak, Eugeniusz Szyr and Julian Tokarski, the ruling Party's Central Committee Secretary Jerzy Albrecht, almost twenty ministers representing different industries, the head of the Economic Department of the PUWP Central Committee, and many industrial and commercial managers. The meeting expressed sharp criticism of the Perspective Plan. The Plan was denounced for projecting an inadequate rate of development and in particular insufficient growth of industrial production. Its authors were accused of professing the bourgeois theory of declining economic growth. Demands for increases in plan targets were again based on assessments of productive capacity, and not on the final use of production. Another pretext for rejecting this version of the Plan was the desire to catch up and even overtake at least one advanced capitalist country in terms of national income, an ambition which was not based on any reliable or consistent economic analysis.[19] Soon after this meeting, in May 1960, Kalecki was removed from his position on the Board of the Planning Commission. This undoubtedly limited his influence on the work of the Commission in general, as well as on the subsequent course of work on the Perspective Plan.

At the beginning of 1960, the Perspective Plan Office drew up *Podstawowe kierunki i proporcje rozwoju gospodarczego Polskiej Rzeczypospolitej Ludowej w latach 1961–75* (*The Fundamental Directions and Parameters of Economic Development in the Polish People's Republic in 1961–75*).[20] This met some of the demands of the Kalecki Plan's critics. The basic difference between this (April 1960) version of the Perspective Plan, and the version outlined in the 'Outline Perspective Plan' (of September 1959) was the higher growth rate of industrial production, with higher industrial output targets set for 1975, especially for heavy industry. The targets for national income and its essential components in both versions of the Plan are shown in Table 4.1.

There are two reasons why a comparison between the main targets of the Perspective Plan in its 1959 version and actual economic performance is difficult. First of all, this version of the Plan was not intended by its authors to be the final draft: on the contrary, it was supposed to be continually revised. Secondly, a fundamental change

Table 4.1 Selected targets for 1975 in the September 1959 and April 1960 versions of the Polish Perspective Plan[a]

Target	1975 *September 1959 version*	*April 1960 version*[b]
Gross national income produced	271.0	291.0
Gross national income distributed	258.0	278.0
Consumption	252.0	264.0
Accumulation	274.0	313.0
Total investment	284.0	321.0
Share of productive investment in gross national income produced in 1975 (%)	19.7	21.9
Share of accumulation in gross national income distributed in 1975 (%)	30.6	32.6
Output of the machine industry	344.0	400–450
Output of the chemicals industry	500	600–650
Steel production (m. tonnes)	14.0	18.0
Electricity supply (bn. kWh.)	90.0	95–100
Cement production (m. tonnes)	18.4	19.0
Average Number of residents per Urban dwelling room (nos.)	1.18	1.20

[a] 1960 = 100 unless otherwise stated.
[b] Some of the differences between the targets are due to changes in the 1960 base quantities used in the different versions of the Plan. Thus, for example, the 1975 volume of consumption was the same in both versions of the Plan, and the increase in the target index was due to a reduced actual level of consumption in 1960. Changes in the main targets for the production of more important articles and commodity categories are given in AKPRM/ZPP ref. 125/20.

in economic policy occurred in the 1970s, towards making much greater use of foreign credits, in particular for investment, while the Kalecki Plan was in principle based on balanced foreign trade. Both of these circumstances should be borne in mind in comparing the more important targets of the Kalecki Plan, and the actual outcome in 1975. This comparison is shown in Table 4.2.

The targets given in Tables 4.1 and 4.2 show that the targets for 1975 proposed in the 1959 version of the Perspective Plan were fairly close to the actual outcome in respect of basic indicators such as gross national income produced and consumption. Plan targets for many commodities such as steel, cement, meat, cereals and sugar were also much the same as their actual output in 1975. However, actual productive investment and the difference between the national income produced and the national income distributed were much higher than projected in the Plan. The Kalecki Plan implied a significantly higher economic efficiency: it had aimed at attaining what was actually attained by 1975, but at the expense of much less investment and without a balance of payments deficit.

According to a popular view, consumption in Poland increases at a slow rate because of a too heavy investment burden. It is claimed, for instance, that if in the period 1961–75 the rate of investment had been less than it actually was, it would have been possible to achieve the same or even higher consumption rate as in 1975. In the light of Table 4.2 and the debate, discussed above, about the determination of growth rates in the Perspective Plan, this view appears to be not entirely correct. In fact, the fundamental cause of Poland's economic failures has been the low and declining efficiency of production and investment. For these reasons, to obtain the level of consumption postulated by Kalecki, greater investment was necessary than was proposed by him. (Although undoubtedly, given the inefficient system of economic management and planning, and with the same political and institutional set-up of the 1970s, many glaringly incorrect investment decisions could have been avoided, and the same consumption growth achieved at substantially lower investment outlays.) Low and falling economic efficiency in Poland has made necessary greater investment outlays per unit of consumption. Were it not for these huge and rising investment rates, consumption growth would have been most probably less than it actually was.

Further work on the Perspective Plan, whose time-horizon was extended to cover the years 1961–80, was limited to mainly technical amendments, substitution of some figures for others and reconciling targets, and re-processing the original set of data. The operation of the Perspective Plan Sub-commissions soon afterwards came to a standstill and the whole undertaking itself, an essentially multi-stage project, was in fact terminated at that stage. Kalecki gradually withdrew from work on the Plan, participating in it partly because, as Chairman of the Polish delegation to the Economic Commission of the Council for Mutual Economic Assistance, he supervised Polish efforts to co-ordinate the long-term plans of the CMEA member states.

THE CO-ORDINATION OF CMEA MEMBERS' PERSPECTIVE PLANS

The question of co-ordinating perspective plans was first discussed by the chairmen of the respective Planning Commissions of the

Table 4.2 Main economic indicators in the 1959 Kalecki Perspective Plan and Polish actual economic performance 1960–75

	Unit of measurement	*1960*		*1965*		*1970*		*1975*	
		Plan	*Actual*	*Plan*	*Actual*	*Plan*	*Actual*	*Plan*	*Actual*
Gross national income produced	%	100.0	100.0	141.7	134.8	196.6	180.1	267.2	287.2
Gross national income distributed	%	100.0	100.0	137.0	133.1	189.9	176.1	256.1	309.5
Accumulation	%	100.0	100.0	137.0	149.4	203.9	205.1	256.1	493.4
of which productive investment	%	100.0	100.0	136.4	153.3	201.8	229.6	262.7	573.9
Consumption	%	100.0	100.0	133.7	127.9	184.4	167.8	248.6	252.9
Dwellings[a]	mlns	15.7	17.3	18.1	19.9	22.1	23.9	28.1	27.5
Employment[b]	mlns	14.4	12.4	15.4	13.5	16.1	15.2	16.9	16.9
of which non-agricultural employment	mlns	7.4	7.0	8.3	8.2	9.3	10.0	11.2	11.7
Machine industry output	%	100.0	100.0	164.7	186.7	240.0	335.3	341.0	671.9
Chemical industry output	%	100.0	100.0	210.0	287.8	340.0	347.7	490.9	621.3
Bituminous coal	mlns tonnes	103.0	104.0	113.0	119.0	123.0	140.0	135.0	172.0
Electricity supply	bn kWh	28.8	29.3	43.5	43.8	63.0	64.5	90.0	97.2
Steel	mlns tonnes	6.4	6.7	9.0	9.1	11.5	11.8	14.0	15.0
Cement	mlns tonnes	6.6	6.6	10.2	9.6	14.0	12.2	18.4	18.5

Table 4.2–continued

	Unit of measurement	*1960*		*1965*		*1970*		*1975*	
		Plan	*Actual*	*Plan*	*Actual*	*Plan*	*Actual*	*Plan*	*Actual*
Timber	mln m^3	16.2	15.9	15.0	16.4	15.0	18.5	15.0	21.8
Cereal production (rye wheat barley and corn)	mlns tonnes	14.4	14.3	16.1	15.5	n.a.	15.4	18.3	18.0
Meat (incl. consumption by farmers)	mlns tonnes	1.8	1.7	2.3	2.0	n.a.	2.2	2.7	3.1
Milk[c]	bn litres	12.3	12.1	15.4	12.9	n.a.	14.5	16.2	15.9
Sugar	mlns tonnes	1.2	1.4	1.5	1.6	1.6	1.4	1.8	1.7
Cotton textiles per capita	metres	21.5	17.9	24.7	19.9	27.6	21.8	32.3	22.3
Woollen textiles per capita	metres	2.8	2.2	3.2	2.3	3.6	2.4	4.2	3.0

[a] Actual figures include empty dwellings and are corrected to take account of an underestimate of the 1960 stock of dwellings.

[b] The differences between planned and actual employment are in part because the 1960 census figures and those from the 1958 population survey were not available in drawing up the plan.

[c] The initial projection for milk production in 1975 contained in the summary and the detailed versions of the Outline Perspective Plan was set at 21.1bn. litres. This was completely unrealistic and Kalecki strongly opposed this figure. Under pressure from him, a more cautious forecast was made, resulting in a lower target for milk production of 16.2bn. litres. This is the figure given above.

Source: Wytyczne do planu perspektywicznego na lata 1961–1975 in the detailed (AKPRM ZPP ref. 79/2) and summary (AKPRM ZPP ref. 79/42) versions, and Roczniki Statystyczne GUS (Statistical Yearbooks)

CMEA member states in Prague, in September 1957. Initially the prevailing view was that such co-ordination should consist of setting out one general perspective plan, which would then be broken down into specific tasks for the individual countries. Kalecki proposed instead that each country should work out its own perspective plan, based on its own needs and economic potential. These plans would then be co-ordinated and modified by the CMEA Economic Commission. The Foreign Trade Commission of the CMEA, in conjunction with its industrial commissions, would examine the possibilities for maintaining the foreign trade equilibrium of each country. Finally, countries would enter into bilateral and multilateral agreements on specialisation and division of labour in particular types of industrial production. The resolution on plan co-ordination that was finally accepted by the meeting largely reflected the views of the Polish delegation.

The Economic Commission of the CMEA was set up at the end of October 1957. Among other tasks the Commission was to undertake studies on perspective plans and their co-ordination. These studies involved comparisons of past economic growth in CMEA countries in the context of economic relations between them and the directions of technological advance in particular sectors and industries and so on. The results were then to be compared with those of similar studies carried out for capitalist countries.

In view of the differences of expertise in drawing up perspective plans, the Economic Commission asked the Polish delegation to set up a working party to draw up an agenda for work on ways of comparing national income accounts.[21] A conference of experts was held in Warsaw in July 1958, at which the differences in national income accounting conventions among CMEA member countries, and the comparison of their respective shares of accumulation and consumption in national income were discussed.[22] In November 1959, a meeting of the CMEA Economic Commission in Moscow approved a joint proposal on national income and expenditure accounting. The proposal was along the lines of the national income accounting system that was first developed in the course of preliminary work on the Polish perspective plan.

Besides these technical matters, Kalecki sought to secure for the Polish delegation the broadest possible participation in the work on division of labour within the CMEA and the principles of intra-CMEA co-ordination of perspective plans to 1975. He argued that this work, albeit theoretical, ought not to have an abstract character but should include practical solutions to the crucial issues of economic co-operation, which should take the form of concluding long-term trade agreements. In his view, primary consideration should be given to the problems of expanding the raw materials base in relation to those countries' needs. At the same time, he emphasised that foreign investment could help in expanding this base where investment was the development bottleneck and not, say, labour shortages or long investment cycles.

Starting in mid-1960, work on co-ordinating the perspective plans of different sectors and industries in the member countries of the CMEA was intensified. This was prompted by attempts to secure consistency in the development of those sectors and industries, and in particular to draw up a preliminary balance of fuel and energy supplies and requirements for the European member countries together. But despite the efforts of the Polish delegation, this work in the Economic Commission never got beyond the bilateral consultations that corresponded to the first phase of perspective plan co-ordination. It seems that the major obstacle was the differences of opinion, not just within the CMEA Economic Commission, but within the CMEA as a whole. Some countries regarded the Economic Commission as an agency for allocating production tasks among individual member countries, without regard for the need to ensure an equilibrium in their respective balances of foreign payments. On the other hand, Poland wanted it to assist in the detailed co-ordination of the perspective plans drawn up by each country. Ultimately, this co-ordination was to take the form of long-term agreements on division of labour and specialisation.

However, although the ultimate aim of co-ordinating perspective plans in the CMEA Economic Commission was not achieved, its methodological work on national income accounting had a fundamental and lasting influence in the socialist countries. Few in Poland or the other CMEA countries are aware that many of the basic concepts which are used in the economic planning and statistical analyses of those countries, were pioneered by Kalecki and his collaborators in their work on the Polish Perspective Plan.

DEBATES ON THE FIVE YEAR PLANS FOR 1956–70

Towards the end of 1956, when the draft Five Year Plan for 1956–60 and the proposed annual plan for 1957 were ready for consideration by the Sejm, a request was made to postpone discussion on the Five Year Plan until the spring of 1957. The request was from Oscar Lange, who was then the Chairman of the Sejm's Plan, Budget and Finance Commission, and the Sejm's *rapporteur* for both plans. The reason for the request was to enable the Five Year Plan to be considered by the newly-elected Sejm, which was to meet for its first session in February 1957, and whose term of office would coincide with the period of the Plan. Moreover, it was hoped that by early 1957 the tensions following the social upheavals of June and October 1956 would have dispersed. Meanwhile, a special team was set up in the Planning Commission to analyse and recommend solutions to the fundamental problems in the 1956–60 Five Year Plan. As we have already mentioned, at the head of this team was Michał Kalecki.

In January and February 1957, the team put forward a number of proposals on general economic policy aimed at increasing the realism of the Plan and its effectiveness. For instance, it was suggested that foreign exchange savings on the purchases of raw materials inputs should be linked to the payment of financial rewards to those achieving such savings. There was also a proposal to allow unplanned investment financed by foreign investors and paid for by the future exports derived from such investment. In particular these were to be investments expanding the output of some of the more attractive raw material commodities. This was in fact the first Polish initiative to make use of foreign investment credits on a self-financing basis. Finally, the team suggested a far-reaching decentralisation of the management of state-owned local industry and producer co-operatives.[23]

At the same time, a lively discussion, in which Kalecki participated, was taking place in the Planning Commission on changes to the 1956–60 Five Year Plan. Kalecki argued in favour of maintaing the increase in living standards at no less than 30 per cent. But he proposed working out an additional programme to raise living standards by a further 5–10 per cent if planned production targets were over-fulfilled and if additional foreign credits were available. He supported a reduction in planned investment and a shift of investment towards the most efficient projects, and criticised the simplistic view that the only obstacle to achieving a consumption target of 30–35 per cent growth was the balance of payments deficit. The difficulties in balancing foreign payments were only a symptom of other development bottlenecks: inadequate supplies of raw materials and the technical and organisational difficulties at different stages of production. It was there, and not just in actual foreign trade that reserves should be sought out. If sufficient of these reserves were mobilised, then a 35 per cent increase in living standards was, according to Kalecki, feasible. However, exceeding this target would require additional imports entailing an increase in an already projected deficit on the balance of payments.[24]

His experience of working on the 1956–60 Five Year Plan influenced Kalecki's outlook during the various stages of drawing up the subsequent 1961–5 Five Year Plan. In particular it was reflected in his insistence on the latter plan's realism and its internal consistency, and his defence of consumption in the short run. The other main factor was his attempts to make the 1961–5 Plan fit in with the 1961–75 Perspective Plan, which was then being drawn up under his supervision.

At the end of 1958, at a conference organised by the Economic Council, Kalecki argued that the slightly slower rate of economic growth postulated in the 1961–5 Five Year Plan (compared with the 1956–60 Five Year Plan), with a somewhat higher share of productive investment in national income, was the outcome of three factors. First of all, there was the preponderance of large investment project start-ups in the 1961–5 period, while in 1956–60 they had been mainly finishing off such projects. Secondly, there was less scope for utilising spare capacity. Thirdly, there was a more pressing balance of payments constraint. For these reasons he thought it hardly possible to accelerate economic growth in 1961–5. Because the 1961–5 Plan postulated a considerably slower growth in consumption than was planned for 1956–60 (the increases in consumption were 25 per cent and 35 per cent respectively), Kalecki argued that increasing the share of investment in national income was out of the question, the more so since in many instances – and especially in expanding the raw materials base – this would meet with serious technical and organisational difficulties. In fact, only certain additional investments with short pay-back periods, which would help to overcome those bottlenecks, would benefit the growth of consumption under the 1961–5 Plan. However, the increase in national income that could be obtained from such investments was less than was widely expected, and therefore Kalecki warned against overestimating these possibilities.

Accelerating economic growth by more intensive use of productive capacity was also not going to be easy. More often than not, it required additional materials that were already in short supply, since the under-utilised capacity was found not in the extractive sector, but in manufacturing industries such as the machine industry. Obtaining additional raw materials from abroad in exchange for increased exports of manufactured goods was in turn constrained by limited export possibilities. In this way, the constraints of the raw materials base and the capacity of foreign markets to absorb manufactured goods were obstacles to speeding up economic growth by mobilising spare capacity in manufacturing.

Finally, the economic growth rate could be increased by savings on either investment outlays or raw materials inputs. Although such possibilities undoubtedly existed, in Kalecki's view they were best taken into account in annual plans rather than in five year plans. This was because the results obtained in a given year could be used as a guide for the following year's targets, whereas if a five year plan overestimated the possibilities of such savings, then this could lead to distortions and inconsistencies in its implementation. In any case, increased material savings were already necessary to secure the fulfilment of the plan's existing targets for economic growth: the potential for raising growth rates by still further savings was therefore severely limited. Furthermore, bearing in mind the efforts that would have to be made simply to achieve planned agricultural output, and the difficulties faced in maintaining full employment throughout 1961–5, Kalecki argued that efforts should be concentrated above all on securing the fulfilment of the Plan targets rather than on raising the economic growth rate.

> The targets for national income and industrial production in 1958–65 are similar to those projected in the Soviet Plan, which has astonished the whole world. As we have already mentioned, the Plan for the coming five years still requires a lot of work to secure solid foundations for its fulfilment. The purpose of this work is the same as with efforts aimed at increasing the growth rate of production. However, the attitude of the planner is different. *The person who aims at raising the growth rate is more easily reconciled to imbalances in particular sectors. But the person who aims above all to secure plan fulfilment seeks out weak points and tries to remedy them; and only later thinks of raising the growth rate.*[25]

Kalecki saw dangerous parallels between the 1961–5 Five Year Plan and the 1950–5 Six Year Plan. The periods of both plans came after years whose circumstances favoured abnormally rapid growth of production. The Six Year Plan came after post-War reconstruction, while the plan for 1961–5 was to follow after the 1956–60 Five Year Plan, whose course was also set in unusually favourable, but unfortunately unrepeatable conditions. This inspired a natural and dangerous tendency to underestimate the difficulties of carrying out plans in subsequent years. Under both plans, these difficulties were exacerbated by the starting up of major investment projects. Thus Kalecki warned that, in similar circumstances, similar mistakes should not be made. Every effort should be made to ensure that the Plan for 1961–5 did not confirm the dismal jest that, history teaches only one thing, and that is that it teaches us nothing.

The main problems in implementing the 1961–5 Five Year Plan were with agriculture, foreign trade, investment and employment. Industrial production, which was originally planned to increase by 52 per cent, and on a comparative basis by around 50 per cent, actually rose by 50.9 per cent. The plan for investment goods was overfulfilled by 12.8 billion złoty, while the plan for means of consumption was underfulfilled by 7 billion złoty. In 1965, the value of total agricultural output amounted to 93.8 per cent of that planned. Of this, the crop harvest nearly reached the level planned, but animal husbandry was 13.8 per cent short of its target. The Plan forecasts for the rationalisation of fodder use, and the reduction of fodder input per unit of output, turned out to be completely unrealistic.

The foreign trade plan had to be revised in May 1961 because of problems in the supply of raw materials from the other socialist countries, and the need to switch to raw materials imports from capitalist countries. The revised plan was overfulfilled on the export side by 5.7 per cent and on the import side by 20.6 per cent. Because of this the planned reduction in the trade deficit was not achieved. Another reason for this was the failure to fulfil the export plan for plant, machinery and transport equipment, where only 93 per cent of the target was reached. Total investment outlays at actual cost, came to 98 per cent of those projected in the Five Year Plan. However, while expenditure on productive investment exceeded that planned by 4.5 billion złoty, non-productive investment fell short of that planned by 17.5 billion złoty. This short-fall was mainly in housing construction. Productive investment exceeded the plan in industry, construction, forestry and trade. But the agricultural investment plan was not completed and total outlays in the economy as a whole (including private agriculture) were 8 billion złoty less than planned. Changes in the investment plan, especially in industry, were caused by serious underestimation of the costs of individual projects, so the actual results obtained were substantially less than the volumes forecast in the plan. All these factors contributed to under-fulfilment of the target for national income, which in the event only increased by 33.7 per cent. Consumption overall rose by only 27 per cent, while personal consumption rose by just 24.7 per cent, as opposed to the 32.1 per cent increase forecast in the Plan.

The greatest departure from the Plan was in the increase in employment. Whereas the target for this in the socialised (that is, co-operative and state) sector was an increase of 735 000 persons, the actual increase came to 1.237 millions, or almost half a million more than planned. To some extent, this was because the actual increase in labour supply turned out to be greater than planned; but this underestimate only accounted for around 155 000 people. The remainder was due to the increase in economic activity rates among women, mainly in urban areas. This large increase in employment in turn had an effect on the fulfilment of the planned increase in the average real wage. This was forecast to rise by 23 per cent over the whole period. In fact, the average nominal wage rose by only 20 per cent. With an increase in living costs of 11.3 per cent, this reduced the increase in the real average wage to a mere 8 per cent.

Economic performance in 1961–5, and the fulfilment of many of Kalecki's pessimistic forecasts, affected his outlook on the 1966–70 Five Year Plan. At the end of 1963, when the preliminary draft of this plan was drawn up, Kalecki was very critical of it: he considered its projected growth rate for consumption to be far too low, especially coming after the disappointing consumption increase in 1961–5. He felt that the average annual growth rate of overall consumption, in its first approximation in the new plan, should be projected at 6 per cent, or 4.5 per cent per capita, and recommended that studies should be made to determine the feasibility of this target.[26]

Kalecki presented his views in 'Uwagi o planie gospodarczym na lata 1966–1970' ('Observations on the 1966–1970 Economic Plan'),[27] which was published in April 1964. In this article, Kalecki revised his earlier suggestion that the annual average growth rate of total consumption should be raised to 6 per cent. Instead, he argued that it should be raised only to 5.5 per cent from the planned 4.8 per cent. This indicates how, in putting forward proposals to accelerate consumption growth, Kalecki was not courting easy popularity, but always sought a realistic assessment of economic possibilities. He knew and often spoke of how difficult it was to raise consumption growth by one percentage point. He also understood very well that this extra percentage growth in consumption was very important, bearing in mind that wages had to rise by 2 per cent per annum just to keep pace with changes in the structure of employment and wage drift. Because of this, it was often just the additional increase in consumption over and above that 2 per cent that was seen by the public as an actual increase in their living standards.

Kalecki also reiterated his earlier suggestion that the capital-intensity of investment should be reduced and that, with a relatively plentiful labour supply, more labour-intensive and capital and raw materials-saving technologies should be selected. He argued for further savings on investment outlays by modernising old plant, rather than building new projects, and also by introducing a four-shift system in new coal and sulphur mines.

Kalecki recommended increasing housing construction by 5 billion złoty, while reducing total productive investment by 20 billion złoty. He regarded the elimination of grain imports postulated in the 'Outline of Polish Development', and the resulting constraint on livestock rearing as mistaken: in his opinion, the target for livestock rearing could be increased in the 1966–70 Five Year Plan from the 11 per cent proposed in the 'Outline' to 16 per cent, the percentage rise in crop production proposed in the 'Outline'. The grain imports necessary to achieve this increase in livestock rearing could be paid for by exporting some of the additional pigs for slaughter. According to Kalecki's calculations, this operation would enable national income in 1970 to be increased by around 3.5 billion złoty.

Materials savings could be increased by setting up a central agency to examine large investment projects and give preference to materials-savings projects. The activities of such an agency could be supplemented by a system of incentives encouraging materials saving and the undertaking by enterprises of small investments designed to obtain such savings. Such an incentives system ought also to prompt materials saving in current production. But here it was necessary, in Kalecki's opinion to replace wherever possible gross production targets by net production targets. However, he warned that all changes in the structure of incentives designed to reduce material inputs would be ineffective unless combined with a fundamental reform in quality control. As long as this depended on the enterprise management, there could be no guarantee that input savings would not be at the expense of output quality.

Finally, regarding export policy, Kalecki continued to have his reservations about the economic gain obtained from the export of complex industrial plants linked to the granting of long-term credits, and the lack of appreciation of the importance of long-term foreign trade agreements. Exports on long-term credit terms did nothing to alleviate current balance of payments difficulties while imposing on the economy the same burdens as investment. Kalecki indicated that trade and the mutual opening up of markets was of greater benefit to developing countries than economic aid.

Although he realised the importance of raising the annual growth rate of living standards by 0.7 per cent, and increasing the total investment in new housing in 1966–70 by 5 billion złoty, this was not the main purpose behind Kalecki's comments on the Five Year Plan. He described this as:

> sketching out an approach to economic planning which aims, in a *realistic* way, to achieve the fastest possible progress in raising standards of living under present conditions, and in a way that is consistent with long-term economic development. The effective application of this approach can, under favourable circumstances, secure even better results than those to which our analysis has brought us. (emphasis added)[28]

The correctness of many of Kalecki's criticisms was confirmed in the course of implementing the 1966–70 Plan, and the results achieved at its conclusion in 1970. It was not only the course of events which proved him right. Immediately after the change of leadership in Poland in 1970, his views were vindicated in the wave of criticism of the arbitrary economic policies of Gomułka and his associates. Many remembered that the only reply to Kalecki's 'Observations', was Gomułka's contemptuous dismissal at the Warsaw Conference of the PUWP: 'Professors with titles, grown-up people, instead of conducting research, or helping, write nonsensical theses.'[29] However, at the time, the atmosphere in the run-up to the Fourth Congress of the PUWP (15–20 June 1964) did not favour independent judgement or attempts to correct the decisions already mapped out in the 'Outline of Polish Economic Development in 1966–1970', and approved at the Fifteenth Plenary Meeting of the Party's Central Committee. But it is nevertheless worth reflecting on the origin of these decisions and their underlying assumptions, which Kalecki fought in vain to modify, as well as on the causes of his failure.

In Polish conditions, an increase in real wages gives rise to an approximately proportionate increase in the demand for meat. A corresponding increase in grain imports for fodder must follow. Thus, the decision to eliminate grain imports in 1966–70 made it impossible to raise the annual growth rate of consumption to 5.5 per cent in that period. The need to eliminate grain imports in turn derived from difficulties in holding down the foreign trade deficit, a factor limiting Polish economic development since the Second World War, and one of the main reasons for the failure to fulfil the 1961–5 Five Year Plan, which aimed to increase foreign exchange reserves. Among the more important factors behind the failure of this foreign trade policy was the lower than planned growth of exports of plant, machinery and transport equipment. Above-plan export of fuel and raw materials was impossible because of difficulties in increasing their rate of extraction. In effect, the fulfilment of the 1966–70 Plan in foreign trade was to be obtained by saving on imports. The import plan for 1961–5 had been overfulfilled by nearly 21 per cent. The export plan was also overfulfilled, but only by around 6 per cent. While imports of plant and machinery were 25 per cent higher than planned, and imports of fuel and raw materials exceeded their plan by around 10 per cent, the import of food and agricultural produce (mainly grain and fodder), was greater than planned by as much as 45 per cent, and that of manufactured consumer articles was 32 per cent greater.[30] Therefore the central planners focused their concern on the growth of grain and fodder imports.

Ultimately it seems that there were three main factors behind the Party leadership's decision to eliminate grain imports. Undoubtedly the decision was a personal initiative by Gomułka himself, and bore his unyielding character, but limiting imports of other commodities might have been expected to result in powerful opposition from various industrial interest groups. However, the beneficiaries of grain imports, that is, consumers and private pig-breeders, had no more or less formal institutions to protect their interests. The decision should also have been opposed by the Ministry of Agriculture, because it limited meat production and the incomes of private farmers, but instead of opposing a clearly erroneous decision, the Ministry occupied itself in seeking out arguments to justify it.

A second factor was a certain neurosis created by the circumstances in which grain was imported. It resulted primarily from unfavourable changes in the credit conditions under which Poland purchased agricultural surpluses in the USA, as a result of which Poland was going to have to pay in the second half of the 1960s in part with ready cash, and in part with 2–3 year credits, creating additional problems in the balance of payments with the capitalist countries. This situation was exacerbated by uncertainty about grain supplies from the USSR in 1965, and the outcome of long-term trade negotiations with the USSR in 1964.

The third factor which ultimately appears to have turned the scales in favour of eliminating grain imports from the Plan was the bizarre notion of dried potatoes. In seeking a rationale for eliminating grain imports, the Ministry of Agriculture put forward the idea of replacing them with dried potatoes. These have a certain amount of protein which can be enriched and used as fodder instead of grain. The idea was criticised by virtually all serious experts on the subject, but it somehow reached Gomułka, who propagated it in his speeches and thereby won its acceptance. Despite the huge domestic resources and foreign currency spent on it, this policy turned into a complete fiasco. It was revised after 1971, and the country reverted to increasing grain imports.

Thus the main reason for the failure of Kalecki's proposal to raise the planned increase in living standards by, among other steps, additional imports of grain amounting to 1.2 million tonnes in 1970, was the unwillingness of the authorities at the time to consider alternative ways of balancing foreign trade.[31] There was therefore only the actual historical process of success or failure to check on the validity of a particular development strategy.

As for investment policy, in practice investment proposals were reduced at the stage of drawing together the plan, although as a rule that plan was then overfulfilled. The Planning Commission was always under pressure from ministries and local authorities, supported by particular members of the government's inner cabinet (the *prezydium rządu*), to increase investment. In the Commission itself sectional industrial pressure in support of particular ministries or local authorities was found as high as the Deputy Chairman level of the Commission. These pressures were reinforced by subsequent organisational decisions that again went counter to advice from Kalecki. This was to create a central institution capable of checking on the particular investment projects put forward by industrial management, and examining alternative schemes for major projects. Instead, it was decided to dissolve the Planning Commission's Chief

Commission for the Assessment of Investment Projects (*Główna Komisja Oceny Projektów Inwestycyjnych*). It was certainly not in the interest of industrial and regional pressure groups to have, as proposed by Kalecki, a central institution to check on the efficiency of the the particular projects that they favoured.

> The change in policy recommended by Kalecki over trade with developing countries met with difficulties because the foreign trade agencies were weak and gave in too readily to the demands of overseas negotiators who wanted to obtain the best possible credit terms. The Ministry of Foreign Trade put forward to the government's inner cabinet successive proposals to grant long-term credits tied to the export of turnkey projects. These were invariably approved, despite the opposition of the Planning Commission.[32]

Finally, regarding quality control, it is worth recalling that Kalecki raised this question many times at various conferences and in many publications. In this case again, a major factor responsible for the failure of this proposal was the lack of any appropriately organised representation of consumers' interests, which could have enforced quality control in a persistent sellers' market.

THE BASIC PRINCIPLES OF LONG-TERM PLANNING

The debates and discussions around successive five year plans in 1956–70, and the experience gained in drawing up the first Polish perspective plan led Kalecki to formulate some basic principles of long-term planning. As always with Kalecki, these principles referred to the actual social and institutional conditions of planning and to the given system of national income accounting.

In analysing the fundamental problems of long-term planning, Kalecki reduced these to a great extent to the selection of the growth rate of national income. He therefore placed especial emphasis on the precise definition of national income. The concept used in perspective planning differed in one major respect from the concept used in capitalist countries. While including 'material services', such as transport, laundries, restaurants and trade, the socialist concept does not include the administrative services of the government, leisure, education, health services, and so on. This concept of national income also excludes services based on fixed capital, such as housing and hotels. In Kalecki's view, such a definition has many advantages from the planner's point of view. It is easier to measure changes over time in the real value of commodities than corresponding changes in services. In the national income accounts of the capitalist countries the real growth of economic activity in, for example, administration, is measured by using index numbers of administrative employment (weighted according to their salaries in the base year). However, this indicator cannot reflect changes in the productivity of administrative personnel. There are also difficulties in including rents for housing in national income, because of the very high capital intensity of housing construction: the average capital output ratio in the economy as a whole, where rents are included as a service output, can be greatly distorted by a high share of housing construction in investment outlays. In Kalecki's long-term planning procedure services were included in employment projections, for example in the case of government employees, and in planning for the satisfaction of consumer needs by means of developing the fixed capital stock used in consumption (for example, in planning the sizes of dwellings). Accordingly, investment outlays are divided up into productive investment – that is, investment contributing to the production of material goods and services – and non-productive investment, which comprises all other fixed capital outlays and includes housing construction.

Referring to the social and institutional conditions of long-term planning, Kalecki clearly stated that such planning can only be effective in a socialist economy. Applying similar methods of planning even to mixed economies would be very difficult indeed. Even in a socialist economy, the rates of growth of particular sectors are limited by technical and organisational factors. Because of them, raising the overall economic growth rate requires increased investment for each incremental unit of output and, beyond a certain growth rate, further acceleration may turn out to be completely impossible. In the mixed economy, Kalecki pointed out, there are additional institutional factors which severely limit the development of certain sectors of the economy. These factors may occur especially in agriculture, where social conditions such as feudal land ownership and the domination of peasants by merchants and moneylenders may hinder the rapid development of production. The resulting slow growth rate of food supplies may impede more rapid economic growth, or else cause price inflation in markets for essential consumer goods.

Another problem which does not arise in the socialist economy, but must be taken account of in a mixed economy, is the management of investment in the private sector. In some key industries, private investment may turn out to be insufficient to meet planned requirements. In other cases, private investment in less pressing sectors (for example, luxury housing) may be excessive and absorb scarce resources needed more urgently elsewhere. Combinations of such circumstances may also obviously occur.

The financing of economic development is also different in a mixed economy from that in a socialist economy. In the latter, the fundamental problem is the contradiction between a high economic growth rate, securing a high level of consumption in the longer term, and the level of consumption in the short run. However, once some acceptable compromise is arrived at in this respect, the problem of investment finance consists primarily of setting the appropriate relationship of prices to wages.

The situation is different in a mixed economy in so far as public investment is financed primarily out of tax revenue. Kalecki considered it unjust to tax the poor as long as there were rich people in society. But the privileged classes and foreign capital can on the whole successfully resist the imposition of additional taxation on them by means of their political influence. Moreover, even if laws to tax them are passed, they can often evade them. 'The result is, in part, the shifting of the burden of financing investment to the poor and, in part, the restriction of the possibilities of accumulation'.[33] The obstacles to long-term planning in mixed economies can be partially overcome. However, Kalecki emphasised that planning in those circumstances should include the preparation of steps necessary to overcome the political obstacles to rapid economic development.

Given a favourable (that is, socialist) political environment, Kalecki distinguished four basic principles of long-term planning. These were:

(1) consistency;
(2) efficiency of planned investment;
(3) plan realism; and
(4) protecting consumers' interests in the short-run.[34]

Except for the last they come close to the known praxeological rules of efficient planning (that the plan should be realistic, internally consistent and operative), which were first put forward by a famous Polish philosopher and praxeologist, Tadeusz Kotarbiński. The importance of Kalecki's principles lies in his re-interpretation and development of these rules, which soon brought him into conflict with many orthodox views.

Plan consistency means for Kalecki not only the need to ensure a plan's internal equilibrium and its realism. He was concerned here with a more general and important issue, namely a method of plan construction which would lead to the avoidance of not only shortages, but also unnecessary surpluses. Therefore his method was one in which planning started off from certain assumptions about the economic growth rate, the future structure of consumption, and its relationship to non-productive investment. In turn, these assumptions largely determined the industrial profile of planned final output and productive investment, as well as the rate of growth for particular branches of the economy.

Kalecki contrasted this approach with the method of starting to draw up the plan by projecting growth rates for particular branches of the economy. These growth rates then determine the overall economic growth rate and, given additional assumptions about the structure of consumption and its relation to non-productive investment, they also give an implicit profile of industrial production and growth rates for particular industries. In general, these will be completely different from the starting assumptions. The resulting shortages may be corrected if the principle of plan realism is observed. However, a tendency may arise to maintain high production targets in the 'surplus' industries, which in turn leads to waste and the unnecessary overestimation of input requirements in the plan, or the creation of unnecessary reserves. The latter in turn may encourage extravagance in the course of plan implementation. Accordingly, Kalecki opposed the notion of industrialisation as an end in itself. Instead he argued that it should be merely the outcome of a long-term economic development plan. Similarly, a rapid increase in machine production should result not from following the slogan of 'mechanisation', but from actual development requirements.

The principle of efficiency of planned investment essentially meant obtaining a given increase in national income by means of the smallest possible investment outlay, while maintaining balance in the labour market and foreign trade. For the smaller the productive investment necessary to achieve a planned increase in national income is, the greater will be that part of the increase which can be allocated to consumption and non-productive investment. Kalecki therefore criticised the tendency to install in new factories equipment of the highest technical specifications, and to save on labour by replacing it with expensive automation. Labour-savings may be achieved in different ways. The capital-intensity of new equipment should be such that the increase in labour productivity would enable labour markets to stay in balance, and allow for the reduction in working hours according to plan. Kalecki did not regard increasing labour productivity as an end in itself, but as an instrument for maintaining full employment at a given economic growth rate. Thus he attached great importance to the modernisation of existing factories. In this way, considerable savings of labour and increases in productive capacity could be achieved often with relatively small investment outlays.

Maintaining foreign trade equilibrium required investment in exporting and import-substituting industries. According to the principle of efficiency of planned investment, Kalecki insisted on carrying out a calculation of the comparative efficiency of obtaining a unit of foreign exchange. In the light of known difficulties in expanding exports, due to limited markets, and the technical and organisational difficulties in developing particular activities (caused by, for example, limited natural resources, difficulties with the recruitment of labour, the long periods needed to adapt some new methods of production) Kalecki laid special emphasis on materials-saving investments, and the production of synthetic substitute materials. He also pointed out that the higher the planned economic growth rate is, the lower the profitability of exports. Ultimately, this tends to limit consumption, and at a sufficiently high economic growth rate it may prove altogether impossible to balance imports with exports.

The principle of plan realism means the realistic setting of various targets in the plan, such as materials useage norms, projected capacity utilisation, planned construction and gestation periods in investment, export possibilities and projected investment costs. 'Mobilising' targets, if unsupported by actual measures designed to make them feasible, for example, investments to save on material inputs, usually mobilise industry to undertake other, not necessarily desirable changes in the composition of output, to reduce its quality, and so on.

> In this way, a 'tight' plan emerges, that is, one that is ambitious, but risky, if not already wholly unrealistic. If such a plan fails, which can happen, than it causes losses. In other words, the

> outcome is worse than if planning had been more cautious. The realism of a plan depends on drawing it up in such a way as to make the risk of non-fulfilment small.[35]

The factor which increases the realism of a plan is its reserves, especially those in particularly 'tight' balances. However, the purpose of reserves should not be to relieve planners of their duty to work out precise targets wherever such targets can be fairly accurately calculated, for example, in commodity balances and investment outlays. Kalecki considered it particularly undesirable to set herculean targets and then set up huge reserves to allow at least in part for their fulfilment. This practice merely obscures the plan, and creates situations in which even large reserves may turn out to be insufficient.

There was yet another factor which in Kalecki's view made the principle of plan realism particularly important.

> The non-fulfilment of an unrealistic plan in the final outcome will affect mainly consumption. This is because there exists a natural tendency to maintain the continuity of investment processes, in order to avoid tying up capital in unfinished projects. However, the losses due to the non-fulfilment of the plan in the consumption sector should not be under-estimated. The demoralisation of the people has not only various consequences for economic activity but also, and by no means less importantly, has a very bad effect on the consolidation of socialist ideals in social consciousness.[36]

The principle of protecting consumer interests in the short run concerns the compromise between consumption in the short and the long term. The greater the projected increase in national income in the plan, the greater will be the planned investments necessary to achieve it. The higher the rate of economic growth, the greater must be the share of productive investment in that income. That is why, although in the long run a faster growth rate in general provides for higher living standards, in the short run this relationship is reversed: a higher growth rate reduces current consumption.

The rate of economic growth in a long-term plan must therefore be the outcome of a compromise between the current and long-term interests of consumers. This is a compromise in which the interests of current consumption should not be neglected.

From these fundamental principles of long-term planning, based on his own experience, Kalecki drew the following conclusion:

> Abiding by the principles of plan realism and maintaining consumption in the near future leads to restraint in setting the growth rate, while the avoidance of waste and the conscientious analysis of investment efficiency allows this rate to be kept, notwithstanding, at a relatively high level.[37]

The experience of the Polish economy in the 1960s and the 1970s unfortunately shows that these principles were far from being observed in practice.

Notes

1. Perspective Plan Office, Archives of the Planning Commission (henceforth AKPRM/ZPP), ref 59/1.
2. AKPRM/2pp, ref. 59/1.
3. See Kalecki, *Dzieła*, vol. III, pp. 416–20.
4. AKPRM/ZPP ref. 59/4.
5. First published in O. Lange (ed.), *Zagadnienia ekonomii politycznej socjalizmu* (Warsaw: Książka i Wiedza, 1958) See also M. Kalecki, *Dzieła*, vol. III.
6. Cf. M. Kalecki, 'The Problem of the Optimum Structure of Consumption', *Mathematical Studies in Economics and Statistics in the USSR and Eastern Europe, A Journal of Translations* (1965), no. 4, pp. 3–16.
7. Published by Główny Urząd Statystyczny (Warsaw, 1966). Independently of this empirical work, what were probably the first studies of the input/output methodology in Poland were undertaken by Paweł Sulmicki. In 1957–8, he gave a number of lectures on the subject in the Economic Studies Institute of the Planning Commission.
8. See 'The 1961–1975 Long-Run Economic Plan', *Polish Perspectives* (1959), no. 3, pp. 3–19, and 'Czynniki ograniczające tempo wzrostu dochodu narodowego w gospodarce socjalistycznej' ('The Factors Limiting the Growth Rate of a Socialist Economy'), *Gospodarka Planowa* (1958), no. 8.
9. M. Kalecki, *Dzieła*, vol. III, pp. 429–34. See also 'Konferencja w sprawie wytycznych planu perspektywicznego PRL na lata 1961–1975' ('Conference on the Outline Perspective Plan for Poland for 1961–1975') *Z Prac Zakładu Nauk Ekonomicznych PAN* (1958), no. 7; *Biuletyn Informacyjny Zakładu Planów Perspektywicznych* (1958), no. 4, AKPRM/ZPP ref. 96/4; Minutes of the Eleventh Plenary Meeting of the Economic Council AURM ref. 545/27/7.
10. 'Sprawozdanie z konferencji w ZNE PAN' ('Report of the Conference of the Economics Institute of the Polish Academy of Sciences') *Gospo-*

darka Planowa (1958), no. 12, pp. 38–9. See also M. Rakowski, 'O tempie wzrostu w planie perspektywicznym' ('On the Economic Growth Rate in the Perspective Plan'), *Gospodarka Planowa* (1958), no. 10, pp. 29–35.

11. 'Konferencja w sprawie wytycznych'. op.cit. The full quotation is given in M. Kalecki, *Dzieła*, vol. III, pp. 435–7.
12. *Materiały XII Plenum KC PZPR* (Warsaw, 1958), pp. 67–152.
13. *Nowe Drogi* (1959), no. 4.
14. *XII Plenum Komitetu Centralnego Polskiej Zjednoczonej Partii Robotniczej* (Warsaw, 1958), pp. 66–7.
15. *Nowe Drogi* (1959), no. 4, p. 517.
16. Ibid., pp. 675–705. See also M. Kalecki, 'Podstawowe zagadnienia planu pięcioletniego na lata 1961–1965' ('Basic Issues of the 1961–1965 Five Year Plan'), in *Dzieła*, vol. III.
17. 'Wstępne koncepcje rozwoju i zagospodarowania województw w latach 1961–1975' ('Preliminary Outlines for the Economic Development of Voivodships in 1961–1975') (Warsaw: 1959) vols I-IV, AKPRM/ZPP, ref. 59/9–14.
18. AKPRM/ZPP, ref. 79/2 and 79/42.
19. Minute no. 3 of the Meeting of the Planning Commission Board on 11 January 1960, AKPRM, ref. 43/3.
20. AKPRM/ZPP, ref. 59/6.
21. Report of the First Meeting of the CMEA Economic Commission AKPRM/ZPP ref. 301/6.
22. AKPRM ref. 301/2
23. M. Kalecki, *Dzieła*, vol. III, pp. 354–6.
24. AKPRM, ref. 5/80, 5/81 and 5/85.
25. M. Kalecki, *Dzieła*, vol. III, p. 260.
26. Minutes of the Meeting of the Planning Commission Board on 6 December 1963, AKPRM, ref. 92/98; M. Kalecki, *Dzieła*, vol. III, pp. 464–5.
27. *Życie Gospodarcze* (1964), no. 15, pp. 1 and 2, and *Dzieła*, vol. III, pp. 285–97. Kalecki formulated his observations very conscientiously with the help of W. Brus, W. Herer and others who tested some of his working hypotheses and postulated relationships. He regarded this as his contribution to the public discussion on the 'Wytyczne rozwoju gospodarczego Polski w latach 1966–1970' ('An Outline of Polish Economic Development in 1966–1970'), which had been approved by the ruling Party's Central Committee.
28. M. Kalecki, *Dzieła*, vol. III, p. 247.
29. W. Bieńkowski, *Socjologia klęski* (*The Sociology of Defeat*') (Paris, 1971), p. 114. Kalecki often said later that it was this reaction by Gomułka that finally persuaded him to leave the Planning Commission.
30. The above-plan imports of manufactured consumer goods came mostly from additional purchases in other socialist countries. In 1964–5, Poland achieved surpluses in current trade with these countries in other commodity groups, and these surpluses were used to augment supplies of consumer goods. Thus, this over-fulfilment was of a different character to that of the rest of the import plan over-fulfilment.

31. Among economists, only Jan Główczyk and Władysław Rydygier supported the elimination of grain imports in their article 'Czy możemy plan wieloletni oprzeć na imporcie zbóż?' (Can we base a Long-Term Plan on Grain Imports?'), *Życie Gospodarcze* (1964), no. 22. Obviously, what was profitable in the mid-1960s was not necessarily so 15–20 years later. From around the mid-1970s the agricultural surpluses and growing protectionism of the EEC's Common Agricultural Policy would have severely limited the profitability of the meat export aspect of Kalecki's proposal.
32. S. Jędrychowski, 'Notatka o współpracy z M. Kaleckim' ('A Note on my Work with M. Kalecki'), quoted in M. Kalecki, *Dzieła*, vol. III, p. 471. Stefan Jędrychowski was Chairman of the Planning Commission from 1956 to 1968.
33. M. Kalecki, 'The Differences between Perspective Planning in Socialist and Mixed Economies', in *Essays on Developing Economies* (Hassocks: Harvester, 1976), p. 29.
34. M. Kalecki, 'On the Basic Principles of Long-Term Planning', in *Selected Essays on Economic Planning*.
35. Ibid., p. 282.
36. Ibid., p. 283.
37. Ibid., p. 284.

5 The Foundations of Growth Theory

THE PROPORTIONS OF SOCIALIST REPRODUCTION

The doctrine of the faster rate of growth of Department I (producing means of production) than of Department II (producing means of consumption), had its origins at the end of the nineteenth century in the debates around the Marxian schemes of reproduction, and the conditions derived from them for balanced expanded reproduction. In these discussions an important role was played by Rosa Luxemburg, with her critique of Bulgakov, Tugan-Baranovski and Lenin, who thought that the faster growth of Department I was a feature only of capitalism, and of Kautsky, who considered that in the long run it was impossible. Rosa Luxemburg argued that the faster growth rate of Department I was a general economic law, operating in all expanding socio-economic formations. Furthermore, she stated that in the socialist economy, the gap between the growth rate of Department I and that of Department II must be even greater than under capitalism. For many years after this assertion provided an unquestioned theoretical justification of the policy of forced industrialisation in the Soviet Union.

Possibly against its author's intentions, Stalin's book *The Economic Problems of Socialism in the USSR* re-opened the question of the proportions of socialist reproduction. In the USSR at the turn of 1954 production was switched towards articles of mass consumption and improved consumer supplies. This created a more favourable climate for questioning the doctrine of Department I's faster growth, and the first attempts by Soviet economists to undermine this dogma were undertaken at this time.

Methodologically, the doctrine was based on two prior assumptions; one about the character of technical progress, and the other regarding the rate of economic growth. In a lecture to the Polish Economists' Association on 20 November 1955, Kalecki distinguished between these two issues, and analysed the effects on the two departments' relative development of various combinations of technical progress and declining, constant and rising economic growth. Kalecki's argument was carefully balanced and avoided any implicit criticism of previous Soviet economic policy. While making no a priori assumptions about the type of technical progress found in practice, it had an enormous practical significance. Even if it did not show the direction of future economic policy in Poland, it did undermine the theoretical foundations for the policy of restraining current consumption in order to force industrialisation.

This lecture became the basis of Kalecki's celebrated speech at the Second Conference of Polish Economists, in June 1956, where it provoked great interest and applause.[1] Kalecki argued there that expanding investment faster than national income would accelerate economic growth, but is only feasible as long as there are labour reserves. After these have been exhausted, the rate of economic growth must return to a level consistent with equilibrium in the labour market. Moreover, the acceleration in economic growth may be halted even before labour reserves are exhausted, because of bottlenecks in the economy. Each speeding up of economic growth requires an increase in the share of investment in national income. Thus, although in the long run faster growth with unlimited labour reserves will have a favourable effect on consumption, the temporary lowering of consumption growth in the short term may discourage such a policy. Kalecki therefore concluded that:

> it is not possible to deduce from the above reasoning a general rule for investment and national income growth. The decision as to whether investment should rise at the same rate as, or faster than, national income depends on such factors as the existence of labour reserves, the prevailing type of technical progress, and whether the highest possible level of consumption in the near future is preferred to its maximisation in the long term.[2]

At the same conference, Bronisław Minc reiterated his earlier reservations about the necessity for Department I to expand more rapidly than Department II. Kalecki's and Minc's conclusions evoked some polemics, but the discussion at the Second Conference of Polish Economists marked the abandonment in Poland of the dogma of the necessity to expand Department I more rapidly than Department II. However, in the other CMEA countries, this doctrine remained the prevailing orthodoxy, and the views of Kalecki and Minc were severely criticised, especially in the USSR and Czechoslovakia.[3] It seems that this debate, by then nearly seventy years old, was only finally closed in 1961, when Oskar Lange confirmed the lack of foundation for this doctrine.[4]

Kalecki's paper of June 1956 also contained the framework of a theory of growth in a socialist economy, starting several studies in this area of economic theory long before the theory of economic growth under socialism became a separate subject of investigation: up to the time of his lecture, the problems of growth under socialism were analysed only in the context of the theory of reproduction, whereas for Kalecki this had already become a distinct field of economic enquiry much earlier.

THE ORIGINS OF RESEARCH ON THE THEORY OF GROWTH OF A SOCIALIST ECONOMY

The Soviet economist G. A. Fel'dman is regarded as the precursor of the theory of growth of a socialist economy. His two-sector model of economic growth drew upon the theoretical heritage of the 1920s, when Soviet economists had to address themselves to the problems of growth in connection with their work on national economic planning.[5] Fel'dman's models were rediscovered in the West in the early 1950s, and a few years later in Poland. In the 1930s and 1940s, the problems of aggregate models of economic growth were analysed by Western economists. But the reliable economic statistics necessary to verify these models and apply them in practice, only became available after the Second World War. Time series data on the volume and structure of national production, capital, employment and trade provided the theory of growth with more solid foundations. The general growth equation for a one-sector economy is:

$$\text{Rate of Growth} = \frac{\text{Rate of Productive Accumulation}}{\text{Capital/Output Ratio}}$$

This was first put forward by Roy Harrod, and subsequently by Evsey Domar.[6] As Bródy has pointed out, the formula was already implicit in Kalecki's paper of 1935.[7] In 1944 Kalecki introduced the notion of an equilibrium rate of economic growth:

> The question of the 'equilibrium' *level* of private investment at which we should aim in the regime of full employment requires

> some preliminary remarks about the concept of the degree of utilisation of equipment, by which we mean the ratio of actual output to the maximum capacity of equipment . . . To maintain the degree of utilisation of equipment the capacity of the latter must expand proportionately to the increase in the working population and productivity of labour. This gives us the clue as to what should be the level of private investment. *Private investment must be at a level adequate to expand the capacity of equipment* pari passu *with the increase in working population and productivity of labour, that is proportionately to full employment output.*[8]

In the early 1950s, Kalecki used an explicit aggregate growth equation similar to the Harrod–Domar equation, in connection with his work on successive *World Economic Reports*, which were prepared under his direction in the United Nations Secretariat. According to Stanisław Braun, a friend and close associate of Kalecki's at the UN Secretariat, Kalecki himself prepared part of the summary of economic development in the socialist countries in 1952–3. In his summing up of this analysis, Kalecki wrote:

> The decline in the proportion of resources allocated to investment which is planned in all countries of the area will tend to reduce the rate of increase in the national product. Indeed, on the assumption of full utilization of equipment, the rate of increase in the national product is proportionate to the share of net investment in the product, if the relation between net investment and the increment in productive capacity remains constant. This will be seen from the following formula:

$$\text{Rate of Increase in National Product} = \frac{\text{Net Investment}}{\text{National Product}} \times \frac{\text{Increment in Productive Capacity}}{\text{Net Investment}}$$

> It follows from this formula that the effect of a reduced share of investment in national product may be partly off-set by policies tending to increase the effectiveness of investment in terms of adding to productive capacity. Such policies have indeed been put into operation.[9]

In his 1955 and 1956 papers referred to above, Kalecki extended this formula to take into account the effect on economic growth of, on the one hand, the losses of productive capacity due to ageing and wear and tear and, on the other hand, of improvements in the utilisation of existing capacity. He subsequently made the relationship between the growth of a socialist economy and investment more specific in a series of articles published in 1957 and 1958, in which he linked the construction period of investment with economic growth and investment, and analysed the effects, on consumption and national income, of shortening the construction period.[10]

As with Fel'dman, the main source of inspiration for Kalecki's subsequent research on economic growth in a socialist economy was his direct experience of economic planning and, specifically, his work on the first perspective plan for Polish economic development in 1961–75. This experience prompted a series of articles which, expanded and made more specific, gave rise to Kalecki's *Introduction to the Theory of Growth in a Socialist Economy*.[11]

Indeed, the Introduction can be interpreted as generalisations about two sets of problems: on the one hand it deals with the methodological problems in economic planning (for example, how to calculate national income and its components, measures of production, prices for aggregation); on the other it also describes a method of determining the rate of economic growth in the plan, allowing for technical and organisational barriers to growth, raw materials supply constraints, problems in balancing foreign trade, and the trade-off between current and eventual future consumption.

During the academic years 1961–2 and 1962–3, Kalecki delivered a series of lectures and seminars at the *Szkoła Główna Planowania i Statystyki* (The Main School of Planning and Statistics, Warsaw's social sciences university, known as SGPiS) on the problems of economic growth in socialist economies. In May 1962 he gave a cycle of lectures and seminars on the same subject at the Social Sciences Faculty of Manchester University. Finally, in September 1962, Kalecki gave two lectures at the Institute of Social Sciences and the Institute of World Politics and Economics in Belgrade, where he presented the conclusions of the *Introduction*, together with a graphic illustration of a 'Government Decision Curve', which he used to explain the procedure for the rational determination by the economic authorities of their target rate of economic growth. Soon after, the *Introduction* appeared for the first time in print.

THE FIRST REACTIONS TO KALECKI'S THEORY

The *Introduction to the Theory of Growth in a Socialist Economy* was the first attempt at a systematic exposition of the determination of the rate of growth of national income in a centrally planned socialist economy, over a time horizon of at least a few years, taking into account three sets of circumstances:

(1) the limitations imposed on the choice of economic growth rates by consumption in the short and long term:
(2) difficulties in balancing foreign trade, which as a rule are exacerbated as economic growth is accelerated; and
(3) the need to overcome labour shortages by intensive mechanisation if the growth rate target exceeds a certain level.

These considerations form the basis of Kalecki's theory. The formal relationships expressed in equations defining increases in national income and its rate of growth, are merely its analytical framework.

The direct growth factors in Kalecki's formal model are the growth of employment, depending upon the natural increase in the labour force, and the growth of labour productivity, which depends upon technical progress. The level of employment and its productivity depends in turn on indirect factors which are summarised in the equation:

$$\Delta Y = \frac{1}{m} . I - a.Y + u.Y \tag{1}$$

where ΔY is the increase in income from the beginning of the time period in question to the start of the next one; *Y* is the level of national income in that period; *m* is the incremental capital/output ratio; *a* is the coefficient of depreciation of capital during the period; *u* is the coefficient representing the increase in national income due to improved use of existing capacity. *I* is the level of investment during the period. *Y* and *I* are expressed in constant prices and without deductions for depreciation.

Dividing by *Y*, we get:

$$\frac{\Delta Y}{Y} = \frac{1}{m} . \frac{I}{Y} - a + u \tag{2}$$

If there are unused labour reserves and by increasing automation, it is possible to obtain a temporary increase in national income over and above that warranted by the direct growth factors. However, this necessitates corresponding changes in indirect factors, that is, raising the share of productive investment in national income, the capital–output ratio, and other parameters of equation (2).

In his analysis, Kalecki was mainly concerned with the transitional acceleration of growth where there are labour reserves and in their absence. Assuming that the acceleration of growth would be to satisfy consumer needs, Kalecki applied here the same premise that underlay for him the determination of the economic growth rate in perspective planning. In either case, the starting point must be to define the extent to which planned growth will satisfy actual consumer needs, while the productive potential of particular industries *defines* the feasible limits of projected growth, but does not *determine* it (see pp. 63–70 above).

The criterion of choice for the planned economic growth rate is a compromise between the consumption forgone in the shorter run for the sake of an increased consumption in the long run. In contrast to solutions based on a Golden Rule of Accumulation, the advantage of Kalecki's approach to resolving this dilemma was that it attempted to accommodate the criteria and principles of decision-making by the socialist central authorities, which would concentrate on transitional processes rather than on equilibrium steady growth paths. Kalecki warned, however, that his concept of the Government Decision Curve must not be treated mechanistically, for it was only intended to illustrate the government's handling of the dilemma regarding how much current consumption to sacrifice for the sake of greater future consumption. It was not intended to absolve the economic policy-makers of their responsibility to take into account various incommensurable economic elements and non-economic political and social factors, public opinion, and so on.

Kalecki's analysis of the relationship between particular growth factors enabled him to introduce into his model the conditions limiting the central planners' freedom of choice of economic growth rate. Kalecki put forward the concept of barriers to growth, which were associated with the tendency of agricultural and extractive industry development to lag behind that of other economic activities, the difficulties of properly controlling and supplying a large number of investment projects and, finally, the problems of balancing foreign trade with limited markets abroad for manufactured commodities.

This approach to growth determination was a major step forward in the political economy of socialism. It enabled economists to get rid of the previously widely accepted notion that economic difficulties in a socialist economy are due to the operation of factors that are wholly foreign to the socialist economy. Kalecki showed that these difficulties need not lie in the existence of a non-socialised sector, neglect of organisation, subjective errors or natural disasters. They may be merely unintended consequences of conscious decisions by the central authorities to accelerate economic growth.

Studying the long-term effects of decisions concerning the rate of economic growth led Kalecki to question yet another dogma of the socialist political economy of those times: for a long time it was thought that raising the share of productive accumulation in national income in the long run must always benefit consumption. Kalecki showed that this need not be the case: in certain circumstances in the absence of unlimited labour supplies, accelerated economic growth can lead to lower consumption growth not just in the short, but also in the longest possible term. Kalecki's theory therefore showed the conditions under which a decision to raise the rate of economic growth would be absolutely irrational from the point of view of consumption in the short and longer term.[12]

Kalecki's approach incorporated a wide range of possibilities but was nevertheless an integrated theory. Added to that was his condensed style of exposition. It is not surprising therefore that his *Introduction to the Theory of Growth in a Socialist Economy* was found difficult to study. Even though it was preceded a couple of years earlier by his paper at the Second Conference of Polish Economists, which contained many ideas developed subsequently in his book, Polish economists were not yet ready to discuss the problems of socialist reproduction in such a language and style, devoid of long quotations from Marx and Lenin, and without repeated emphasis on the superiority of the socialist system over the capitalist one. The above-mentioned lectures at SGPiS gathered crowds of economists of all generations who were interested in economic theory and attracted by Kalecki's worldwide reputation. Yet these lectures only marginally contributed to a better understanding of his theory: only a few of his students overcame the difficulties of following the lecturer's thoughts and stayed to the end of his course.

At that time there gathered around Kalecki a group of economists about half of whom were his colleagues from the Planning Commission and the Economic Council. The remainder of them were mainly staff at Warsaw's university institutes. This group undertook intensive research and teaching to develop and broaden the appeal of Kalecki's theories. Two seminar groups started regular meetings: one on Third-World economic development, and later another one on the theory of growth in a socialist economy. The latter was run jointly by Kalecki and Kazimierz Łaski. From this there emerged the nucleus of a 'Kalecki school'. In addition to a study group on business cycles in contemporary capitalist economies, which had started earlier at the Economics Institute of the Polish Academy of Sciences, there was a group of economists working on development economics, at the core of which was a seminar on the problems of economic development, and a number of economists working on socialist economic growth theory associated with the Kalecki Łaski seminars.

The Kalecki Łaski seminars started in the autumn of 1964 and continued meeting until the end of the 1967–8 academic year. Each year some thirty economists participated in its meetings, of whom half attended it throughout the seminar's existence. The school of thought that emerged from it was distinguished from other schools of thought on the subject primarily by the close links between its growth theory and the basic principles of long-term planning. It also shared Kalecki's commitment to the serious treatment of increasing the living standards of the population as the main aim of economic activity under socialism.

The seminar's members absorbed Kalecki's growth theory relatively quickly. There was also some fascination among them with its applicability as an analytical tool in resolving various practical economic problems. Outside these circles, however, Kalecki's theory was not easily absorbed. Despite widespread recognition of its importance and originality, for a long time the *Introduction* had only three reviews and hardly encountered any criticism. In 1966 Kalecki was awarded a First Class State Prize for the book, and a year later, the book won the Oskar Lange Prize of the Society of Polish Economists. On the occasion of the State Prize award, two reviews of Kalecki's work appeared, outlining in particular his analyses of economic growth in capitalism and in socialism. One more review of the second edition of the *Introduction* completes the list of its reviews published in Polish journals.

Nevertheless, Kalecki's theory soon found itself in many Polish textbooks on the political economy of socialism. Even in the years 1968–73, when it was sharply criticised, it kept a prominent position in the books written or edited at the time by some of his most ardent critics. This widespread and possibly unrivalled textbook success of Kalecki's theory contributed probably as much to its propagation as the activities of the 'Kalecki School'.

The author of the first foreign review of the *Introduction* was Alfred Zauberman of the London School of Economics. In a detailed presentation of Kalecki's theory, he emphasised its methodological originality and scientific importance. Referring to the limiting character of some of its assumptions (especially that of constant prices in transitional processes) Zauberman stressed its deep roots in the economic realities of centrally administered economies. One weakness of the theory was, in his opinion, the lack of any link-up between the theory of growth and the assumptions regarding the way in which the economy functions. (This weakness had been pointed out earlier by a Polish reviewer.) Despite these weaknesses, Zauberman considered Kalecki's theory to be 'a milestone in the literature on the subject'.[13]

The Russian edition of the *Introduction* appeared in Moscow in 1970 with a preface by one of the most prominent Soviet economists and a member of the Soviet Academy of Sciences, Professor T. S. Khachaturov. This preface seems to indicate that Soviet academic economists were prepared to receive Kalecki's theory with reserve, and even coolly. Khachaturov treated the *Introduction* as an eclectic analysis, and accused it of failing to prove the superiority of the socialist economy over capitalism.[14] Khachaturov's opinion was partially balanced by a favourable review in the journal of Soviet mathematical economists which, however, only had a narrow readership.

In Czechoslovakia, interest was quicker and more widespread, but again mainly among non-university economists. This was apparently associated with the considerable economic difficulties experienced in Czechoslovakia at the start of the 1960s, and the hopes of some economists that Kalecki's theory might enable them to determine the causes of the failures in economic policy. These economists were mainly from the Czechoslovak Planning Commission and the Economics Institute of the Czechoslovak Academy of Sciences.

The revised Polish edition of the *Introduction* appeared in English in 1969 (published by Basil Blackwell, republished by CUP in 1972). Between 1969 and 1973 the book was widely presented and reviewed in English language economic journals.

Among the first Polish responses was a certain critical reaction, not so much to the *Introduction* itself as to its equation for economic growth, which Kalecki had already advanced in his 1956 paper and used in his work on the Polish perspective plan. It is worthwhile examining this line of criticism more closely since later on it was widely used and vulgarised in attacks on Kalecki's theories after March 1968.

Kalecki's model of growth in a socialist economy is a vintage-type model. Like all models of this kind it is a multi-sector model in the sense that the total increase in national income depends on factors affecting the change in national income produced in each generation of plant and equipment. However, in the basic equations for economic growth (see above, p. 102), the link between the increase in national income and the changes in employment and the productivity of the labour working on particular generations of plant and equipment, does not appear explicitly. This omission was the reason why Józef Pajestka called it a 'single-factor, investment model of economic growth'.[15] In fact Kalecki's model does include labour as a growth factor. In its first formulations, available labour reserves appear as a limiting factor:

> a rate of growth of investment that is faster than that of national income leads to a faster rate of economic growth. This strategy is feasible provided that some reserve of labour is available. But after it has been exhausted, the rate of growth is bound to fall back to a level appropriate to the current balance in the labour market.[16]

However, in the model presented in the *Introduction* Kalecki revised his approach and used two equations to determine the rate of economic growth. In addition to the earlier equation, slightly modified to take into account changes in circulating capital (stocks and reserves), there now appeared a second equation defining the rate of growth as a function of the growth of labour productivity, α, and the growth of employment, β. Simplifying somewhat, he put forward this equation as $r = \alpha + \beta$. Kalecki saw the mutual dependence of these growth equations as follows:

> Thus, the rate of growth of national income r is determined jointly by α which depends upon technical progress and β (which depends upon the natural rate of growth of the labour force). On the other hand, given the parameters m, k, u and a, the rate of growth r

determines the constant share of accumulation, i, in national income, which is necessary in order to sustain it, on the basis of the equation:

$$r = \frac{1}{k} \cdot i - \frac{m}{k} \cdot (a - u) \qquad (3)^{17}$$

where k is the 'capital – output ratio for total capital' and is equal to the sum total of the incremental capital-output ratio, m, and the incremental inventories–output ratio, μ, and i is the share of productive accumulation in national income. Rearranging, we get:

$$r = \alpha + \beta$$

$$i = r.k + \frac{m\,(a - u)}{k} \qquad (4)$$

The first of these equations defines the rate of growth on the basis of labour supply and productivity growth, while the second defines the share of productive accumulation in national income necessary to achieve this r.

Equation (3) enables us to analyse directly the effects on the time-path of national income and consumption of raising the rate of economic growth through the elimination of unemployment and through accelerating productivity growth by mechanisation. Kalecki was more concerned in his *Introduction* to analyse these problems. This may explain why he preferred to use equation (3) rather than its rearranged form in the set of equations (4). However, since (4) is only a formal representation of the quotation from Kalecki cited above, the error of the assertion that the model is 'a single-factor, investment model of economic growth', which does not take into account labour as a factor of production, is apparent.

THE WAVE OF CRITICISM IN 1968–73

Research on the theory of growth in a socialist economy flourished in Poland from the middle of the 1950s to the end of the 1960s. Kalecki's theory was only one among many. At least three other approaches were differentiated by their methodology and scope. These were the aggregate, the multi-sector, and historical-descriptive models of growth.[18] This fruitful period of research was broken off at the end of the 1960s. (Studies on the historical process of economic growth were already a target for non-scientific accusations a couple of years earlier). In 1968, Kalecki's theory came under an uninhibited wave of attacks, which also spread to other research endeavours.

The main source of economic strains, and the consequent political tensions in the 1960s (whose culmination was the unrest of 1968–70) was the abandonment at the start of the decade of attempts to carry out fundamental economic reforms, aimed at giving enterprises greater autonomy and developing workers' self-management. This manifested itself in the change of political climate around the Economic Council, followed by its disbandment in 1963, and the neutralisation of the workers' council movement a few years earlier.

On the face of it, these circumstances might have strengthened Kalecki's position. At the time he attached possibly even greater importance to limiting the arbitrariness of economic decision-making by the central authorities, and to the creation for them of conditions for rational choice, than to fundamental changes in the system of economic planning and management. In reality, however, the reverse was the case. He was defeated over the methodology and the main targets of the 1960–75 perspective plan, and forced to resign from his job in the Planning Commission in 1964.

Meanwhile, the lack of organisational changes, combined with the absence of any mechanisms for effective social control, and accumulating economic difficulties, all promoted further arbitrary economic decision-making and dogmatic methods of management by the central Party and Government apparatus. In this situation, its response to any economic thought going beyond an apologetic function in relation to the decisions of the authorities (let alone trying to correct them and limit their arbitrariness) was a forgone conclusion from the middle of the 1960s. Kalecki's moral integrity and his 'indisposition' to persons highly placed in the apparatus of authority was well-remembered. His views, for example on the irrationality of eliminating grain imports, attracted harsh disapproval, although without mentioning his name. It is also no coincidence that after March 1968, persons closely associated with the authorities started vigorous, organised criticism of Kalecki's theories, accusing him, among other things, of not being a Marxist.

The social tension and student disorders of March 1968 were the result of many factors, including non-economic ones. From the beginning of the 1960s, dissatisfaction and frustration were expressed about the methods and policies of the authorities towards culture and research. Opposition towards the authoritarian way in which Gomułka and his associates governed emerged in the ruling Party apparatus itself. At the same time, in the Government and Party machinery, there was a revival of demands to 'cleanse' it of 'alien elements'. In these circles, an aggressive 'anti-Zionist' campaign started in the second half of 1967. Without entering into an analysis of these various political factors and tendencies, it should be stated that neither Kalecki nor any of his associates at the SGPiS were directly involved in these disputes and factional antagonisms.

The campaign to break up centres of independent economic thought and eliminate their leading representatives started from a conference organised by the Central Party School of the PUWP's Central Committee.[19] In a paper introducing the discussion, W. Iskra accused Kalecki's model of being 'a twin copy of the Harrod–Domar model'. Like the latter two authors, Kalecki was 'confined by capital fetishism, ignoring the elementary fact that, despite appearances, the fundamental factor of production is not capital but the human being, the direct creator of material goods'. He also criticised Kalecki's model for having an 'a-structural character'.[20]

Another participant, B. Rudowicz, advanced the thesis that after 1956 a number of Polish theoretical economists:

> in full awareness and premeditation undertook efforts to obliterate the differences between bourgeois and marxist economics . . . Models were created with a high degree of formal theoretical precision, that were equally applicable to capitalism as to socialism, which must bring much comfort to our opponents. This comment applies in particular to the theory of growth in a socialist economy. In my judgement, the theory of growth as published by some of our theoreticians does not fulfil either a productive or ideological function. If it is possible to detect any ideological function in it, it is probably . . . to soften up socialism.[21]

Other participants expressed similar sentiments, and it was proposed to organise future conferences to

> reveal and analyse particular false concepts and attitudes in current political economy, indicate neglected problems requiring concentrated research efforts and provide an opportunity to draw up a constructive programme of economic research.[22]

This resolution was carried at a meeting of the Executive of the Polish Economist's Association in a discussion introduced by Józef Pajestka.[23] This was followed by a conference at the SGPiS, where Kalecki and many of his associates were employed, on 17–18 June.

The subject of the conference organised for 17 and 18 June by the Rector and the School's Party Committee, was 'Główne problemy ekonomii politycznej oraz jej nauczania' ('The Main Problems of Political Economy and Teaching It'). The debate was started by presentations of four papers. The first two were by Dymitr Sokołow, 'Problemy stanu i rozwoju ekonomii politycznej w Polsce Ludowej' (Problems of Political Economy and its Development in Poland), and Janusz Górski, 'Problemy teorii wzrostu gospodarki socjalistycznej' ('Problems in the Theory of Economic Growth under Socialism'), and both were devoted to Kalecki's theory of growth. Both presentations elaborated upon a critical assessment of Kalecki's theory given earlier by the local Party authorities.[24]

Without distinguishing between Kalecki's theory of growth in a capitalist economy and his theory of socialist economic growth, Sokołow criticised him for not allowing for long-run supply constraints on production in a capitalist economy. He reproached Kalecki for the 'investment character' of his theory of socialist economic growth. But he mainly found fault with Kalecki's closer associates who, instead of winning over to Marxism this scholar brought up in the 'progressive wing of bourgeois economic thought' had 'capitualated in the face of a stronger scientific personality'.

Janusz Górski concentrated his attention on the theory of growth in a socialist economy, taking as the butt of his attacks a book by Kazimierz Łaski, *Zarys teorii reprodukcji socjalistycznej* (*An Outline of a Theory of Socialist Reproduction*). Not long before, in a review of the book, Górski had emphasised its many merits and Łaski's skilful and bold use of modern research methods. At the end of his review, he wrote that it constituted 'a good theoretical generalisation of many economic phenomena, as well as the basis for many practical decisions'.[25] Now Górski criticised Łaski and Kalecki for a lack of appreciation of the Marxist origins of contemporary growth theory. Kalecki in particular was accused of 'not indicating as well the relationship between his intellectual construction and those of Harrod and Domar, formulated in 1947–58, a few years earlier therefore than Kalecki's growth formula'.[26] Furthermore, Górski criticised Kalecki's theory for its alleged excessive formalism and a lack of realism and potential for empirical verification and practical application, a declining marginal usefulness in its further development; succumbing to bourgeois economic influences, lack of analysis of the social factors and conditions of growth in a socialist economy, and detachment from the theory of how a socialist economy functions.[27]

Concluding, Górski stated that:

> A complete theory of socialist economic growth, like Marx's theory of growth, cannot limit itself to a formal and ahistorical analysis of general growth functions presented exclusively from the point of view of an investment model of growth. [Kalecki's model was anachronistic and] . . . this kind of quite mechanistic reasoning leads in fact to a lack of appreciation of the fundamental growth factor – human labour'.[28]

At the end of his paper, Górski suggested that the social determinants of labour productivity under socialism should be explained in a general theory of growth. Empirical research on a number of topics should be undertaken to test the abstract hypotheses of the theory, and economic studies in Poland should be reorganised in order to enable such research to proceed.

Kalecki firmly rejected this critique. If Sokołow's supply-based model of capitalist economic development, which he had contrasted with Kalecki's demand-based model, was indeed an example of Marxist analysis, then, Kalecki said,

> I do not aspire to this kind of Marxism, which obscures the contradictions of monopoly capitalism. The essence of Marxism consists of elucidating these contradictions. From 1933 to 1968, I worked on explaining them. In 1954 I showed how they were naturally resolved in a socialist economy. I did not close my eyes to the way in which government expenditure, especially on armaments, overcomes contradictions under capitalism, and I showed that these contradictions are in no way removed automatically, but as a result of struggles between monopolies and their representatives.[29]

He argued that the analogy which Sokołow put forward in his paper between Kalecki's theory and those of Keynes and Domar was erroneous. In contrast to his own theory, Keynes did not distinguish between investment and investment decisions, and it was his own theory that showed that capitalists' profits, rather than some nebulous propensity to save, that was the mainspring of economic decisions.

Regarding Górski's accusation that he had concealed the origin of his basic growth equation, Kalecki said

> First of all, the formula is so straightforward that I do not consider it to be a new discovery on whose pedigree it is necessary to expatiate. It is simply an identity expressing the balance of the increase in productive capacity. I introduce this formula on 1½ pages out of a book of 120 pages. The subsequent analysis is completely different from either reproduction schemes or Harrod–Domar models. The latter are concerned with the capitalist system and are therefore supply and demand models, while my approach is only supply analysis. Moreover, in my theory investment and capital-output ratios are expressed gross. But even in the case of supply and demand models of the Harrod–Domar type, I would not need to cite them for the reasons put forward by Professor Austin Robinson in an article in the *Economic Journal* in March 1947.[30]

In replying to the question of whether aggregate theories of growth could still be of any use, Kalecki replied:

> In accordance with what I have written, I consider that the theory of growth in a socialist economy will be of broad scope and complexity. What I have put forward up to now is tentative and incomplete. There is a suggestion that reasoning which concludes that an acceleration in economic growth requires an increase in the share of productive investment in national income is anachronistic. I consider this suggestion to be erroneous. In fact it is this formal argument that enables the assertion which Górski advances without support on p. 20 of his paper to be proved.
>
> But the assumption about increasing labour productivity and coefficient u, which is put forward later on, is entirely arbitrary. It results in an increase in labour productivity on paper only. If this productivity can be increased, why has this not been done before now? It was precisely because I exposed such voluntarism, manifested in raising targets on paper, that I had to leave the Planning Commission. In the reasoning presented on p. 20 of Górski's paper, no account is taken of foreign trade. Allowing for this factor could fundamentally alter the conclusions.[31]

Kalecki also categorically rejected the suggestion that his theory was detached from real life. If one is not to be arbitrary, then assumptions about the growth of labour productivity must be based on the development of science and education. That too requires outlays. The results of these outlays should also be examined. Such an analysis ought to constitute an integral part of the theory of growth. It would make the formal model more complex, but would draw it even closer to reality. He considered that the existing model ought to be continually extended and improved precisely in those directions, rather than rejected, thus allowing free range for arbitrary decisions.

Kalecki devoted the last part of his address to rebutting criticism of the views of W. Brus and J. Tepicht. The first had been accused of advocating extreme economic decentralisation, while the second had allegedly been too cautious in rejecting the notion of agricultural collectivisation that had been forcibly implemented in the 1950s. According to Kalecki, the characteristics of extreme decentralisation were price fixing by enterprises for their own output, which in practice means monopolistic competition, full enterprise discretion over their wage bills and profits, and completely decentralised investment decision-making ultimately leaving only the total investment outlay regulated. Since Brus' model had none of these features, and did not vary much from official policy in respect of them, Kalecki saw no reason for making Brus into a decentralising demon.

The same applied to Tepicht's views. Paradoxically, no one in Poland in the 1950s had undertaken a more trenchant criticism of the concept of collectivisation. Indeed, Kalecki argued that had Tepicht wanted to go further, he would have had to cite what had happened in the years of the Six Year Plan (1950–5) in the Soviet Union, Bulgaria, Romania and so on: in March 1968, this would merely have supplied additional pretexts for personal criticism of him.

There was no discussion on the merits of these views expressed by Kalecki; such was not the aim of the conference anyway. However, its institutional effects appeared very rapidly in the breaking up of the circle of economists which Kalecki had gathered around himself. Kazimierz Łaski was dismissed from the SGPiS, together with several other close collaborators and pupils of Kalecki and Łaski. At the beginning of October 1968 Kalecki submitted his resignation from his post at the SGPiS in protest, and this was accepted. From April 1968 to January 1970 he resigned or was dismissed from a number of other academic institutions and editorial boards of learned journals.

A few months later, the wave of criticism of his theory petered out, but at the turn of 1973 it reappeared: this time the pretext was the good performance of the Polish economy in 1971 and 1972, with industrial and agricultural production, investment, foreign trade and personal incomes substantially exceeding planned projections. The abundance of those two years and a simultaneous acceleration of investment and consumption growth, seemed to confirm the criticism that 'Kalecki's investment theory' did not take sufficient account of the role of the human factor in the growth process.

However, this success gave rise at that time to a phenomenon that Kalecki had always warned against: years of exceptionally good results for the economy, which were caused by a coincidence of favourable but fortuitous circumstances, rather than long-term development trends inspired an impetuous wave of 'hurrah-optimism' in setting development targets. For months the daily press, as well as *Życie Gospodarcze* and *Nowe Drogi* (the main economic weekly and the Party's theoretical journal respectively), conducted a discussion as to whether to project an annual economic growth rate for the next twenty years of 10 per cent (or at a minimum 7 per cent).[32]

On this background, A. Krawczewski put forward a critique of the whole basis of Kalecki's theory. Referring to the then widespread support of Pajestka's view that investment outlays also stimulated consumption in the short run, Krawczewski argued that at a certain stage of development in the relations of production in a socialist economy, the contradiction between investment and current consumption disappears completely. In Krawczewski's opinion, Kalecki's mistake consisted in failing to take into account the fact that 'investment pays for itself'. Once this is realised then it is possible to explain the simultaneous growth of investment and consumption, and understand the illusory nature of the contradictions emphasised in his theory by Kalecki.[33] The mistake in Krawczewski's critique consists in mechanistically translating to the socialist economy the relationship that had already been observed by Kalecki in the early 1930s between investment and consumption in advanced capitalist economies operating at less than full capacity. There the size of national income is determined by effective demand, including demand for articles of consumption. Krawczewski had overlooked the fact that in the socialist 'shortage' economy it is supply factors that largely determine the level of national income.

However, the criticisms advanced by Krawczewski and Rurarz indicate that the direction of attacks upon Kalecki's theory had now changed: whereas in 1968 he was held to be responsible for over-investment in the Polish economy, conjuring up a 'Moloch of Investment', now he was accused of excessive caution in this respect. Needless to say, neither the *Introduction to the Theory of Growth in a Socialist Economy*, nor any of his other writings substantiate any of these accusations.

This criticism of Kalecki's theory from 1968 to 1973 appears to have been pre-arranged, inspired by extra-scientific motives, and aimed at discrediting the scholarly authority of Kalecki himself and his closest associates. Having achieved its immediate goal, the criticism rapidly faded away. The fact that this campaign was led by academics is evidence of weaknesses in the recruitment procedures in Polish higher education and research. This in turn promotes methods of research which have little in common with scholarship. This activity also had long-term adverse effects in that it broke the continuity of theoretical analysis, and checked the development of the scholarly disciplines affected by these purges, including the theory of growth in a socialist economy.

Apart from the personal reasons for the attacks on Kalecki in 1968, associated with his principled and uncompromising approach to scholarship, there was another reason for them: Kalecki had a habit of continually revising and improving his conclusions, and publishing the results which he had obtained at a given time. He was not especially attached to the positions that he had once taken, but offered them up for further analysis. However, these subsequent revisions were often overlooked by his critics. This does not only apply to the modifications which he introduced into his growth model: the same thing happened with his classification of technical progress: many years after the publication of a new and fundamentally different scheme of classification, it was still possible to come across analyses which ignored this change and attributed to Kalecki an approach which he himself had long since abandoned.

This backwardness of Polish economics was even more widespread and acute during the 1970s. When the Polish economy was plunged into its deepest crisis since the Second World War, reflections on theeconomics of the 'advanced socialist society' (*rozwinięte społeczeństwo socjalistyczne*) dominated the economic writing of the time. Among the outstanding pioneers of this literature were some of Kalecki's fiercest critics who, in 1968, had accused him of making his work abstract, excessively formal, and detached from the realities of the Polish economy.

Another reason for the inadequate understanding of Kalecki's theory, and hence false accusations based on misunderstandings of it, was the way in which he presented his ideas. Had the *Introduction* started with equations explaining how national income is produced (that is, making national income a function of the levels of employment and labour productivity as a first approximation), subsequent misapprehensions could perhaps have been avoided. In such an approach, an equation for labour productivity could have been introduced at the next stage. This would have to be defined by the level of the techniques available (that is, by the position of the production curve at any given time), the production techniques (that is, their capital–output ratios), and the know-how and skills of managers and workers. In Kalecki's vintage model this could be one suitably dated equation, or a set of equations, one for each capital vintage. These factors would certainly be included in such a model since they are already implied in particular parameters of Kalecki's original model. However, they may escape notice if, like Kalecki, we concentrate on the dynamics of the economy, and not on its static position in a given point of time. For in proceeding towards economic dynamics an equation for national income is also required, but it is a different equation, representing rather how national income is distributed than how it is generated. This example merely illustrates Kalecki's non-didactic method of exposition. The inclusion of the proposed equations into his model would add nothing new to it. However, their absence gave rise to many misunderstandings and misrepresentations of his theory.

Let us finally deal with that line of criticism of the 1968–73 period, which echoed the point already raised by W. Brus in 1959, that Kalecki's theory missed the feedbacks between economic growth and the system of economic management. This is a complex question to which we shall be returning later on. Let us consider just one aspect of it, referred to at the time in accusations against Kalecki, that his theory encouraged the authorities to undertake excessive investment.

In fact, Kalecki warned against over-investment by emphasising the various constraints and 'barriers' to accelerated growth, the inevitability of a slowing down in the growth of current consumption when the rate of economic growth is raised, and the uncertainty of the benefits for consumers in the long run of such a strategy. He stated this during discussions on long-term plans, and in his many writings where he taught his readers how to examine the aims and instruments of economic policy. Yet all his ideas were based on a deep conviction that the authorities in a planned economy, in theory at least, can make rational macro-economic decisions and carry them out. This 'centralistic' point of view is apparent in Kalecki's growth theory too. It was only towards the end of his life that he considered re-examining the question as to whether the capacity for rational macro-economic decision-making is in fact an immanent feature of a socialist economy. Thus, contrary to the assertions of some of his critics, Kalecki's formulation of the theory of growth in a socialist economy refers to a somewhat idealised system, rather than to the 'undeveloped and highly imperfect socialism of the 1950s'.

It is not clear whether proper political relations are a sufficient condition for rational macro-economic decision-making. It seems certain, however, that such rationality is impossible in a system which is composed of official political relations which are meaningless, and unofficial or extra-statutory ones which are of fundamental significance since they enable various pressure groups and interests to decide behind the scenes on the distribution of income and allocation of resources. Such relations do not allow the central authority to be guided by true social priorities, nor to have the capacity to carry out its decisions. Instead, such a system creates pressure for over-investment exceeding the economy's potential and leading to imbalances in many areas of the economy.

As we have seen, Kalecki was not concerned with these aspects of the way in which a socialist economy operates. However, this did not bother his critics: their ultimately rather vague accusations were about something else. Some were dissatisfied because he did not make facile generalisations about the superiority of socialism over capitalism; others because he did not include in his analysis the 'human factor' of an increasingly educated workforce, the effects of scientific and technical revolutions, the structure of investment, and finally changes in the system of economic planning and management. As we shall see below, this criticism of Kalecki, although not without foundation, consisted primarily of various *desiderata* addressed to him. It did not therefore add much to the development of his theory, or replace it with a better one.

FURTHER DISCUSSIONS

In the first half of the 1970s, a number of attempts were made to develop Kalecki's growth theory or to construct a new one based on different approaches.

W. Iskra tried repeatedly to increase the number of growth factors and arrange them differently from the way in which they operate in Kalecki's model. He created a so-called 'energy and raw materials' economic growth formula but it was shown to be based on circular reasoning and had several other weaknesses.[34] A 'labour growth model' announced by Iskra at the end of the 1960s, which was to oust and supersede Kalecki's model, turned out to be little different from the latter, while the changes introduced in it were widely criticised.[35]

Kazimierz Secomski argued in favour of expanding Kalecki's classic model. During the 1970s, he suggested including in the economic growth equation not only the growth of material production, but the increase in social, cultural and other non-material services. He also proposed to allow for structural and qualitative developments affecting economic growth. In addition to investment in material production, he suggested taking into account non-productive investment. Non-investment factors in economic growth (represented in Kalecki's equation by co-efficient u), were to be expanded and made more specific in modernisation and renovation of the economic infrastructure, the stimulation of innovative enterprise and the introduction of technical and organisational progress, the international division of labour and the economic integration of the CMEA countries, improvements in the system of economic organisation and planning, and other factors of modern economic development.[36] He also argued for a partial optimisation approach with respect to the above factors.

However, there are several difficulties in carrying out these proposed changes, and Secomski himself admits to some problems with them. These are mainly connected with measuring the intensity of the effects of individual factors. For example, how is the contribution of 'modern growth factors' to overall growth to be evaluated, let alone observed? Is it possible to optimise them? Similar problems arise in practice in attempting to measure directly and indirectly the contribution of non-productive investment to economic growth.

A different approach to the theory of economic growth was tried by Józef Pajestka. He argued for the rejection of traditional growth theory, based on the analysis of particular growth factors, in favour of a systems theoretic analysis of models whose aggregate behaviour would be determined by the interaction of their parts.[37] Although it would be difficult at this stage to regard Pajestka's reflections as a complete model of economic growth, it is possible that they may lead in future to the construction of such a model. In relation to Kalecki's theory, Pajestka maintained his earlier criticism that the theory was too narrowly investment-based. In addition, he accused it of excessive formalism, and a failure to take into account social factors, and the 'human factor' in particular.[38] In this context, Pajestka writes:

> Returning to our scheme of interrelated development, it should be pointed out that the effect of the distribution of expenditure on economic growth cannot be understood in the sense that only that part of expenditure which is devoted to investment contributes to economic growth. The part allocated to consumption also contributes to it especially, but not exclusively, through its influence on the human factor. In algebraic growth formulae based on investment as the main growth factor, the higher the rate of investment, the faster is economic growth . . . Fundamental characteristics of the classic model for understanding the interrelationships of the development process are attributing decisive significance to the link between investment and the growth of production, treating consumption as a resultant effect, which comes out beyond the development model . . . It would be more appropriate to state that *increasing the satisfaction of human needs contributes to economic progress and is a necessary condition for it, rather than that it is a sufficient reason for it.*[39]

In so far as this is a criticism of Kalecki's theory, it misrepresents that theory. For instance, in Kalecki's model, consumption is not a 'resultant' variable. Nor does our study confirm that Kalecki did not appreciate the feedback effects from increases in the standard of living to the growth of labour productivity, and the state of what he himself called 'socialist awareness in society' (see p. 92). The main differences between Kalecki's and Pajestka's approaches can be reduced, simplifying somewhat, to differences in the objective function that their respective theories postulate for a socialist economy.

In Kalecki's theory, the objective function is the level and growth path through time of consumption over a given period. In effect, in his paper at the Second Conference of Polish Economists in 1956, and subsequently in his *Introduction*, Kalecki put forward consumption as the basic aim of economic activity under socialism, in place of economic growth, industrialisation, and so on. This change in the objective function was reflected in the clear and unequivocal analytical division of national income into that part of it which is consumed, which was the purpose of economic activity, and that part which was accumulated, and thereby was the means to the realisation of that purpose. Hence the importance which he attached to 'transitional processes' and the significance of his formalisation of the choice of the rate of growth, in the form of the 'government decision curve'.

In many subsequent critiques of Kalecki's theory, there appeared a renewed concentration on the rate of economic growth itself, and even a certain fetishism of it. If we leave aside their verbal declarations, we find at the centre of their interest not the human being as the subject of history, nor even personal consumption as the purpose of economic activity, but the 'human factor' as the most important factor in economic growth. Consumption is obviously also important but, in these approaches, its importance is primarily in so far as it contributes to economic growth. 'Investment in human capital' is important not in itself but primarily because it increases the effectiveness of this most important growth factor, and so on.

The economic strains of the second half of the 1970s, culminating in the Polish economic crisis of the 1980s, prompted Józef Pajestka to revise somewhat his views on the relationship between investment and consumption. Presenting his own diagnosis of the causes of the economic policy errors in the 1970s, he wrote:

> A battle was also fought over the share-out [of national income] between the central authorities and society, which we have previously described as a conflict between the development mission of the authorities and the consumption aspirations of the population. For a while it appeared as if both sides were winning: investment was rising rapidly, as well as earnings and various social benefits. Historical experience showed us that this was not so: both sides were losing, and the nation lost.[40]

Another course of research inspired by Kaleckis' theory is represented by studies aimed at a better integration of this theory with the analysis of the functioning of the socialist economy. This work was systematically conducted during the 1970s by C Józefiak.[41] The same author undertook a pioneering attempt in the literature of the socialist countries to define the maximum permissible level of foreign debt for centrally planned economies, using Kalecki's model.[42] Together with Jan Mujżel, he also put forward an interesting re-interpretation of Kalecki's concept of 'barriers' to economic growth.[43]

Abroad in the 1970s, Kalecki's theory was elaborated by many of his pupils and former associates. Kazimierz Łaski used Kalecki's model in a thorough examination of the usefulness of the neoclassical growth model and investment programming for the theory and practice of planning in a socialist economy.[44] Stanisław Gomułka took up the problem of technical progress in Kalecki's model, disaggregating it to take into account not just the chronological age of particular vintages of productive equipment, but also their technological age.[45]

THE EMPIRICAL TESTING OF KALECKI'S MODEL

The first empirical verification of the model put forward in the *Introduction* was obviously in the confrontation between Kalecki's perspective plan for 1961–75 and the actual economic outcome of those years. There was a close coincidence between economic development as projected in that plan, and actual economic performance, despite some quite fundamental changes in economic policies during the 1970s (see pp. 71–3 above). This shows that the model, when properly used, can serve as a practical instrument for economic planning and forecasting.

In the mid-1960s a number of attempts were made to verify Kalecki's model, not as a forecasting model, but *ex post*, using it to explain actual growth in the long term and the quantitative contributions of particular factors to the overall rate of economic growth. The 1960s also saw the rapid development of economic and statistical studies of this kind. Most of them, in the West as well as in the socialist countries, used simplified production functions of the Cobb–Douglas kind. The first attempts to use Kalecki's model in this type of analysis were made in Czechoslovakia, where the model was used as an alternative to Cobb–Douglas and similar production functions which inspired many methodological and other reservations.

In generalising his experience of perspective planning into his outline of growth theory, Kalecki integrated micro-economic elements of his model (for example, productive investment in particular industries, the capital-output ratios in particular activities, the increase in different stocks and reserves, various non-investment improvements in efficiency) into overall economic aggregates. It therefore became necessary, in testing the model empirically, to disaggregate some of his general categories.

The Czechoslovak economists J. Goldman and J. Flek were primarily interested in isolating the effects of changes in the system of economic management and planning on the rate of economic growth. This enterprise was in part associated with attempts at economic reforms in Czechoslovakia at that time. They disaggregated the coefficient in Kalecki's model representing the effect of non-investment growth factors, u. They separated out the effects of this set of factors, more narrowly defined, as well as the influence of unnecessary increases in stocks and reserves, and that of unspecified factors causing cyclical fluctuations in investment and production in a socialist economy.[46]

Another Czech economist, V. Nachtigal, went in a similar direction, disaggregating the coefficient of the increase in stocks and reserves. He distinguished in it the ratio of the increase in productive reserves to that of national income, μ_1, and the ratio of unfinished investment to national income, μ_2.[47] After introducing these modifications, Nachtigal and Goldman and Flek used Kalecki's model to analyse economic growth in Czechoslovakia in 1950–60 and 1950–65 respectively.

The outcome of these experiments was rather unsatisfactory. In turn this proved to be a set-back to further similar studies.[48] This can only be partially explained by the scepticism with which Kalecki's closest associates in the 1960s regarded the methodological validity of disaggregating the overall rate of economic growth into particular components. Among them, as among the circle around Keynes in the 1930s, interest in constructing theoretical models was not strongly linked to attempts at their empirical verification. However, while in the 1930s Kalecki tested statistically many of the Keynesian theory's propositions, the statistical verification of Kalecki's growth theory was left undeveloped in the 1960s. This lack of empirical testing, combined with the failure to explain fully the shortcomings of the pioneering Czechoslovak studies, rebounded on Kalecki's theory in

1968. Among the criticisms of it that were then advanced was one that

> the advocates of Professor Kalecki's model have not undertaken any empirical attempt to check it against data on the economy . . . Such attempts were made in Czechoslovakia, albeit without much success. It should be made clear if the shortcomings of this verification were the outcome of inept analysis, or the unsuitability of the model itself for empirical testing.[49]

Soon after, the very possibility of statistically testing Kalecki's model was questioned as part of the same wave of criticism.

At the same time, the critics of Kalecki's 'one-sided, purely investment-based' approach advocated the analysis of the effects of various growth factors using the methodology of the American economist E. F. Denison. But the results of such analyses were meagre in comparison to the hopes that were invested in them. It proved impossible to work out a method of measuring the factors in such a way as would not arouse serious methodological doubts. This also gave rise to scepticism about the actual results obtained, which only contributed marginally to a knowledge of reality.[50]

It was only later on that Mieczysław Nasiłowski made some interesting attempts to test statistically Kalecki's equations. The purpose of these studies was to estimate the effect of increases in productive capacity on the potential rate of growth of net output in socialised industry. This potential growth rate was obtained from the investment projects completed in a given year. The difference between it and the actual growth rate was then reduced to deductions from the potential growth rate, due to the completion of projects later than the beginning of the year in which they are operative, and their less than full capacity utilisation, and additions to the potential growth rate resulting from projects approaching full capacity utilisation, but completed prior to the period in question. According to Nasiłowski, only on the basis of such an expansion of the investment term in Kalecki's growth formula is it possible to estimate the effects of the so-called non-investment factors as a residual in the rate of growth of production or national income.[51]

This analysis, and subsequent research by J. Goldman, provided a better grounding for Kalecki's model.[52] However, as with the earlier studies of Goldman, Flek and Nachtigal, Nasiłowski concentrated only on a few selected elements in the Kalecki model. It seems that only when the results of these partial studies are brought together will it be possible to test Kalecki's equations properly in a disaggregated form.

DIRECTIONS FOR FURTHER RESEARCH

In empirical research, it is obviously essential to synthesise the sectoral work done on various elements in Kalecki's equations, and verify them using long-term time series data on national income, productive capacity, investment, employment, and so on. But in what direction should theoretical developments of his model go? For the most part, this direction is already marked out by the criticism addressed to the model. However, that criticism itself has certain weaknesses in its enumerative character and its lack of any independent attempts to fill in and correct the gaps and rectify the mistakes that it claims to have perceived.

Kalecki's growth theory or, more strictly and in accordance with his own views, the outline of this theory, arose in opposition to the hurrah-optimistic approach that saw a sufficiently high rate of accumulation as the means to realise even the most ambitious plans to increase living standards. Kalecki showed that, if the planners's objective function really is the growth of *consumption*, then not every strategy accelerating the growth of national income must benefit consumption in the long run. Moreover, it is not necessary to accept every strategy for raising the economic growth rate even if it promises benefits for consumption in the long term. It is always necessary to set future benefits against current costs. Any conclusion that arises from such a calculation must depend on a political assessment of the relative value of raising or decreasing consumption today and tomorrow.

This is the central theme of the *Introduction*, as it was the central problem in assessing economic development policies in Poland during the 1950s, and in defining their theoretical foundations later on. In formulating and solving this problem lay the strength as well as the weakness of the *Introduction*. The assumptions and analytical tools that Kalecki deployed in this book were developed by him in order best to serve its central theme, and not the problems of socialist economic growth in general, or the actual problems that revealed themselves many years later. For example, Kalecki was convinced that the socialist economy has virtually unlimited possibilities of expansion, but he never studied this issue. In the later 1970s, the rate of economic growth in the socialist countries slowed down, a recession that became especially acute at the turn of the 1980s. In analysing the causes of this, a reading of Kalecki's *Introduction* turns out to be of little help in determining whether we are dealing with a long-term trend (and what are its causes), or whether this is the outcome of the internal conditions of socialist reproduction, or of external conditions in the capitalist economy, the world raw materials and energy crisis, and so on (or a combination of some or all of these factors). These issues, tied up with the long-term possibilities of and barriers to socialist economic expansion, are not investigated in Kalecki's *Introduction*, nor in his other works. It is also unclear whether his analytical model can be successfully adapted to the study of these problems.

A second set of problems which is not found in Kalecki's analysis, but which is associated with the previous one, is how the theory of growth in a socialist economy links up with development theory; that is, how economic growth is tied in with regional development, structural problems, the social distribution of income, environmental protection, and so on. In some of Kalecki's studies (generally not those directly concerned with the problems of economic growth) it is possible to find some signposts on the direction of his thinking about particular issues, which indicate that he was aware of their significance (see Chapter 7). But he did not concern himself systematically with the problems of socialist economic development.

More intensive studies aimed at integrating the theory of growth with development theory were undertaken only in the 1970s. These tried to use analytical tools taken from systems theory, and the concepts of entropy and negentropy. This work, however, is still in its infancy. Some economists have attached great hopes to systems theory, seeing in it a useful way of codifying the main economic variables and relationships. But the first theories of socialist economic growth based on systems analysis (and rejecting the causal relationships postulated by Kalecki) have their own serious limitations. The conclusion that in a system of interlinked elements, everything interacts with everything else, whatever the number of discrete elements seems somewhat trivial. Each element that is identified in such a system becomes a growth factor. Without introducing what are in the nature of things arbitrary criteria of division into primary, secondary and other factors, a causal analysis of growth becomes, on this approach, impossible. But perhaps it is not necessary to throw out the baby with the bathwater. Maybe Kalecki's theory does not need to be altogether rejected in order to construct a theory of socialist economic development. If the questions raised by his theory and the answers it has offered remain valid, perhaps it is possible to construct a theory of development in which Kalecki's growth theory would be an integral part.

Up to now we have been dealing with very wide-ranging problems which are not found in the *Introduction*, and indeed could not be found in it, since (at best) the theory that it contains could only be a part of a more general theory devoted to explaining these problems. But the *Introduction* is also based on two very specific assumptions which, although related more to growth theory than the theory of socialist economic development, nevertheless have important consequences for the latter. Maintaining these assumptions distances Kalecki's theories from the problems which currently have the decisive influence on the growth of socialist economies. The first of these is the technical progress function; the second concerns the motivations and behaviour of economic decision-makers: both are intimately interlinked.

In Kalecki's theory, technical progress is an exogenously determined factor. The distance between isoquants of production in time t and time $t+1$ may change with the capital-intensity of production (this constitutes the criterion for identifying various types of technical progress). But regardless of the kind of technical change, the question remains of what determines the distance between the production curves. If we reject the assumption that technical progress falls uniformly like 'manna from heaven', then we are faced with two fundamental questions. First of all, we have to define a function which would link the rate of innovation in socialist enterprises with the stream of new inventions. The latter in turn would need to be linked to the level of expenditure on basic and development research and patent and licence purchases and so on. (Indeed, Kalecki spoke about the need to introduce this into his growth model during a conference at the SGPiS in 1968.) Secondly, it requires a definition of the conditions under which, broadly speaking, the 'demand' for new inventions would meet the supply of them.[53] These are the conditions which would link the attitudes of enterprises towards technological advances, with the reward system in enterprises, the ways in which they are supplied with fixed and circulating capital, credits and labour, and the rules governing state intervention in the production and investment activity of enterprises. In other words, the way in which technical progress proceeds would have to be integrated with the ways in which enterprises operate.[54]

At this point, the problems of growth again link up with the problems of how an economy functions, and they require the lifting of Kalecki's second assumption. This is that the way in which an economy functions in a given period is a neutral factor in relation to the growth of labour productivity, technical progress, and so on, on the one hand; and to the rate of increase in employment, on the other hand; or, if not, that it merely affects coefficient u. Undoubtedly this assumption requires revision, in particular in the light of the experience of the European countries of the CMEA since the 1970s. A more profound analysis of the relationship between the growth of the socialist economy and the way in which it functions, considered as an integral part of a socio-political whole and its institutional arrangements, is an important and urgent direction for further research to develop Kalecki's classical growth model. These issues increasingly attract the attention of many economists approaching them from the angle of growth problems, as well as those who approach them from the point of view of problems in the way in which the socialist economy functions and the analysis of the general characteristics of that economy. Despite this, the integration of growth problems with the issues of functioning in a socialist economy seems still to be a matter for the future.

Notes

1. This appeared in O. Lange (ed.), *Zagadnienia ekonomii politycznej socjalizmu* (*Problems of the Political Economy of Socialism*) (Warsaw: Książka i Wiedza, 1958) A later version of this appears in M. Kalecki, *Dzieła*, vol. III, pp. 171–84 and in English in M. Kalecki *Selected Essays on Economic Planning*.
2. M. Kalecki, *Selected Essays on Economic Planning*, pp. 82–3.
3. In Czechoslovakia at the begining of 1956, F. Oliva entered a critique of the view that Department I should grow more rapidly than Department II in his article 'Pomjer rostu narodniho produktu a narodniho dochodu' ('Rates of Growth of National Output and National Income'), *Planovane Hospodarstvi* (1956), no. 1.
4. O. Lange, *Theory of Reproduction and Accumulation* (Oxford/Warsaw, 1977).
5. Fel'dman's model is described in E. Domar, 'A Soviet Model of Growth', in *Essays in the Theory of Economic Growth* (Oxford University Press, 1957). Fel'dman's models do not in fact imply any necessity for the faster expansion of Department I.

6. R. F. Harrod, *The Trade Cycle* (Oxford, 1936); E. Domar, 'Capital Expansion, Rate of Growth and Employment', *Econometrica* (1946), no. 1.
7. M. Kalecki, 'A Theory of the Business Cycle' *Review of Economic Studies*, London 1936–1937 vol. IV No. 2 pp 77–97. A Bródy *Proportions, Prices and Planning: A Mathematical Restatement of the Labour Theory of Value* (Akadémia Kiadò, Budapest, 1970).
8. M. Kalecki, 'Three Ways to Full Employment', in *The Economics of Full Employment* (Oxford University Institute of Statistics/Basil Blackwell, 1947), p. 47.
9. United Nations *World Economic Report 1952–1953* (1954), p. 44. In a footnote to this equation, Kalecki explains that, since on the right-hand side of the equation the numerator of the first fraction is the same as the denominator of the second fraction, the formula boils down to an equation between the growth of productive capacity and the growth of aggregate output. This equation therefore implies full capacity utilisation.
10. M. Kalecki, 'The Influence of the Construction Period on the Relationship between Investment and National Income, and the Coefficient of Capital Tied up in Construction' and 'On the Coefficient of Capital Tied up in Construction', in *Selected Essays on Economic Planning*.
11. See M. Kalecki, *Selected Essays on the Economic Growth of the Socialist and the Mixed Economy* (Cambridge University Press, 1972). A close link between his approach to the theory of growth under socialism and socialist long-term planning is also reflected in the title of a paper which Kalecki was to present to the Third Conference of Polish Economists, in 1960: 'Teoretyczne zagadnienia wzrostu gospodarczego na tle polskich doświadczeń planistycznych' ('Theoretical Problems of Economic Growth in the Context of the Polish Experience of Planning'). In fact, the conference did not meet because the authorities expected the economists attending it to use the occasion to criticise the economic policy of the government and its tardiness in introducing economic reforms.
12. This has been shown also by the Golden Rule of Accumulation theorists and Kalecki was later criticised for his 'unnecessary originality' in this respect.
13. A. Zauberman, 'A Few Remarks on Kalecki's Theory of Growth under Socialism', *Kyklos* (1966), no. 3, p. 422.
14. A Polish translation of this introduction, and Kalecki's correspondence on this matter are given in M. Kalecki, *Dzieła*, vol. IV, pp. 259–64.
15. See J. Pajestka, *Zatrudnienie i inwestycje a wzrost gospodarczy* (*Employment, Investment and Economic Growth*) (Warsaw, 1961), pp. 33–4.
16. M. Kalecki, *Selected Essays on Economic Planning*, p. 77.
17. M. Kalecki, *Selected Essays on the Economic Growth of the Socialist and the Mixed Economy*, pp. 24–5.
18. C Józefiak, 'Problematyka wzrostu gospodarczego' ('Problems of Economic Growth'), in 'Stan i zadania nauk ekonomicznych' ('The Condition and Tasks of Economics'), *Ekonomista* (1981), no. 6, p. 1144.
19. In view of the repetitive and descriptive character of the arguments exercised in this wave of criticism, we shall put them forward in chrono-

logical order, showing their common features, but primarily their new elements and accusations not previously adduced. A modicum of research would show that many of Kalecki's critics at that time echoed Khachaturov's accusations against him.

20. 'Sytuacja w ekonomii politycznej socjalizmu' ('The Situation in the Political Economy of Socialism'), *Materiały i Dyskusje* no. 1 (Warsaw: Centralna Szkoła Partyjna przy KC PZPR, 1968), pp. 23–4.
21. Ibid., pp. 44–5.
22. Ibid., p. 52.
23. J. Pajestka, 'Na nowym etapie postępu' ('At a New Stage of Progress'), *Życie Gospodarcze* (1968), no. 22.
24. This is shown by a report by the Committee of the Party organisation at the Foreign Trade Faculty of the SGPiS to a general meeting on 9 May 1968. The relevant quotation from this report is given in M. Kalecki, *Dzieła*, vol. IV, p. 273.
25. J Górski, 'Teoria wzrostu gospodarki socjalistycznej' ('The Theory of Growth in a Socialist Economy'), *Polityka* (1966), no. 8.
26. J Górski, 'Problemy teorii wzrostu gospodarki socjalistycznej' ('Problems of the Theory of Growth of a Socialist Economy') Conference Paper mimeo, p. 6. This accusation was invalid in so far as, in 1964, at a conference of the Political Economy Faculty (*Katedr Ekonomii Politycznej*) of the SGPiS at Zakopane, Kalecki stated outright that the growth equation which he used for the socialist system was a development of the Domar equation. He also indicated the similarities and differences between his formulation of growth factors in a capitalist economy, and those of Harrod and Domar, as well as Marxian reproduction schemes. Ironically, this was in the course of the discussion on a paper by Janusz Górski himself. (See M. Kalecki, *Dzieła*, vol. II (Warsaw, 1980), pp. 587–8). Later on, in a review of the English edition of the *Introduction* in *Kyklos* (1971), no. 1, p. 150, Roy Harrod also pointed out that Kalecki modified the Harrod/Domar equation without reference to the original formulation. For Kalecki's view on this, see p. 113.
27. This last criticism had been advanced earlier by Włodzimięrz Brus (for example, in 'Wzrost a model' ('Growth and the Model'), *Życie Gospodarcze* (1959), no. 2, and following him other economists concerned with these matters. Thus it is paradoxical that it was precisely those economists who were now charged with the responsibility for the inadequate integration of socialist economic growth theory with the theory of its functioning.
28. J. Górski 'Problemy . . .', pp. 17 and 19.
29. M. Kalecki, *Dzieła*, vol. IV (Warsaw, 1984), p. 276. Kalecki's speech, brought together from his own notes, is given in this fourth volume of his Collected Works on pp. 275–80.
30. Ibid. p. 277.
31. Ibid., pp. 277–8. Kalecki's own theory does not entirely explain what determines the size of and changes in coefficients u and α.
32. See, for example, Z. Rurarz, 'Przesłanki przyspieszenia rozwoju kraju' ('The Conditions for Accelerating the Country's Development'), *Nowe*

Drogi (1972), no. 10, and the same author's 'Jeszcze pół procenta' (Half a Percent More'), *Życie Gospodarcze* (1974), no. 12.

33. A. Krawczewski, 'Błędy teorii – korekta praktyki' ('The Errors of Theory and the Corrections of Practice'), *Życie Gospodarcze* (1972) no. 49, and 'Modele a historia' ('Models and History'), *Życie Gospodarcze* (1973), no. 43. Similar criticism of Kalecki's theory was advanced by W. Iskra, 'Teoria wzrostu gospodarczego w podręcznikach ekonomii' ('The Theory of Economic Growth in Economics Textbooks'), *Nowe Drogi* (1972), no. 12, pp. 88–9. Krawczewski was criticised by M. Nasiłowski in 'O rzekomych blędach teorii socjalistycznej akumulacji' ('On Alleged Errors in the Theory of Socialist Accumulation'), *Życie Gospodarcze* (1973), no. 2, and J. Osiatyński in 'Sprzeczności między inwestycjami a konsumpcja' ('The Contradictions Between Investment and Consumption'), *Życie Gospodarcze* (1974), no. 13.
34. W. Iskra, 'Czynniki surowcowo-energetyczne' ('Raw Materials and Energy Factors'), *Życie Gospodarcze* (1973), no. 13. This was criticised by C. Józefiak in 'Czynniki surowcowe a teoria' ('Raw Materials Factors and Theory'), *Życie Gospodarcze* (1973), no. 26.
35. W. Iskra, 'Czynnik ludzki w rozwoju gospodarczym krajów socjalistycznych' ('The Human Factor in the Economic Development of the Socialist Countries') (Warsaw, 1974). See also M. Nasiłowski, 'Zastosowanie formuły M Kaleckiego do analizy wzrostu gospodarczego' ('The Use of Kalecki's Formula in the Analysis of Economic Growth'), *Ekonomista* (1975), no. 5, p. 1031.
36. K. Secomski, *Elementy ekonomii politycznej* (*Elements of Political Economy*) (Warsaw, 1972); 'Nowoczesny rozwój społeczno-ekonomiczny a klasyczny model wzrostu gospodarczego' ('Modern Socio-Economic Development and the Classical Model of Economic Growth'), *Ekonomista*, (1975), no. 5; *Polityka społeczna-ekonomiczna – Zarys teorii (Socio-Economic Policy: An Outline of Theory)* (Warsaw, 1978).
37. J. Pajestka, *Determinanty postępu: Czynniki i współzależności rozwoju społeczno-gospodarczego* (*The Determinants of Progress: The Factors and Interrelationships of Socio-Economic Development*) (Warsaw, 1975); and 'Na marginesie "teorii wzrostu gospodarczego" ' ('On the Margins of "The Theory of Economic Growth" '), *Życie Gospodarcze* (1976), no. 1.
38. J. Pajestka, *Determinanty postępu*, pp. 29–32, 66–7 and 257 ff. For a criticism of this part of Pajestka's analysis and his reply to it, see W. Herer and W. Sadowski, 'Teoria wzrostu gospodarki socjalistycznej w obliczu nowych problemów' ('The Theory of Economic Growth in a Socialist Economy Faces New Problems'), *Życie Gospodarcze* (1976), no. 1. Similar charges of excessive formalism had earlier been levelled by J. Górski in 'Teoria wzrostu'. For earlier criticism of Kalecki's alleged failure to take account of the 'human factor' see the reference to Pajestka on p. 107, above and W. Iskra, *Czynnik ludzki*, pp. 34–5.
39. J. Pajestka, *Determinanty postępu*, pp. 66–8.
40. J. Pajestka, *Polski kryzys lat 1980–1981: Jak do niego doszło i co rokuje* (*The Polish Crisis of 1980–1981: Its Causes and Consequences)* (Warsaw, 1981), p. 90.

41. C. Józefiak, 'Uwagi o związkach między wzrostem gospodarczym i systemem funkcjonowania gospodarki socjalistycznej' ('Observations on the Connections between Economic Growth and the Functioning of the Socialist Economy'), duplicated typescript 1975; 'Warunki pobudzania pozainwestycyjnych czynników wzrostu gospodarczego' ('The Conditions for Stimulating Non-investment Factors of Economic Growth'), *Ekonomista* (1976), no. 5; 'Funkcjonowanie a wzrost' ('Functioning and Growth'), *Życie Gospodarcze* (1977), no. 27.
42. C. Józefiak, 'Opłacalność inwestycyjnych kredytów zagranicznych' ('The Profitability of Foreign Investment Credits'), *Ekonomista* (1979), no. 3.
43. C. Józefiak and J. Mujżel, *Reprodukcja w gospodarce socjalistycznej* (*Reproduction in a Socialist Economy*) (Warsaw, 1974).
44. K Łaski, *The Rate of Growth and the Rate of Interest in the Socialist Economy* (Vienna–New York, 1972). 'Les importations de capitaux et d'equipements et la croissance dans les pays socialistes', *Revue d'Études Comparatives Est-Oeust* (1979), no. 4; 'Uber das Wachstumstempo der Abteilung I und II', in *Sozializmus, Geschichte und Wirtschaft: Festschrift für Eduard Marz* (Vienna, 1973).
45. S Gomułka, 'Inventive Activity, Diffusion and Stages of Economic Growth', *Monographs of the Institute of Economics* (Aarhus, 1971), no. 24; 'Do New Factories Embody Best Practice Technology? New Evidence', *Economic Journal* (1976), no. 4; 'Growth and the Import of Technology: Poland 1971–1980', *Cambridge Journal of Economics* (1978), no. 2.
46. J. Goldman and J. Flek, 'Model hospodářského rűstu za socialismu a kritérium efektivonostii soustavy planovitého řizeni', *Plánowné Hospodářstvi* (1966), no. 3; 'Economic Growth in Czechoslovakia: Experimental Application of Kalecki's Model to Czechoslovak Statistical Data', *Economics of Planning* (1966), no. 2. See also J. Goldman, 'System planowania i zarządzania a wzrost gospodarczy' ('The System of Planning and Management and Economic Growth'), *Życie Gospodarcze* (1965), no. 7. However, the assumptions implicit in Goldman's models are in fact very different from those of Kalecki's model.
47. V. Nachtigal, 'Modifikace základni rovnice v Kaleckého rűstovém modelu socialisticke ekonomiky rozloženim koeficientu μ', *Politická Ekonomie* (1966), no. 8.
48. In the autumn of 1966, Kalecki's growth theory seminar discussed the Goldman and Flek study. Various shortcomings were found in it, including those of linear regression techniques. For Kalecki's view see his letter to Goldman in *Dzieła*, vol. IV, pp. 289–90.
49. J. Górski, 'Problemy teorii wzrostu', p. 23.
50. For a criticism of Denison's method and a defence of Kalecki's see W. Herer and W. Sadowski, 'Kapitałochlonność i postęp techniczno-organizacyjny' ('Capital-intensity and Technical and Organisational Progress'), *Życie Gospodarcze* (1970), no. 19 and J. Osiatyński, 'Ile i dlaczego' ('How Much and Why'), *Życie Gospodarcze* (1970), no. 18.
51. M. Nasiłowski, 'Rozwinięta formuła M. Kaleckiego a idea modelu pracy' ('Kalecki's Formula Expanded and the Idea of a Labour Model'), *Ekonomista* (1973), no. 4; *Analiza czynników wzrostu gospodarczego PRL*

(*An Analysis of the Factors of Economic Growth in the Polish People's Republic*) (Warsaw, 1974); 'Zastosowanie formuły M Kaleckiego do analizy wzrostu gospodarczego' ('The Application of Kalecki's Formula to the Analysis of Economic Development'), *Ekonomista* (1975), no. 5.

52. J. Goldman, 'The Rate of Investment in the Context of the Kalecki Model of Economic Growth under Socialism', in *Economic Growth and Resources, Trends and Factors*, Proceedings of the Fifth World Congress of the International Economic Association, Tokyo 29 August–3 September 1977, vol. II (London, 1980).
53. In fact, in improving the efficiency of productive processes and introducing improvements in the quality of output in the course of production, distinguishing between 'supply' and 'demand' factors makes little sense. In such cases, the way in which the economy functions will determine the enterprise's interest in innovation at all stages.
54. Stanisław Gomułka has been studying both consequences of removing from Kalecki's theory the assumption that a given rate of technical progress is exogenous. See n. 44.

6 Calculating the Efficiency of Investment

FIRST ATTEMPTS IN THEORY AND PRACTICE

Up to the mid-1950s, work on the theoretical foundations of investment efficiency calculations in Poland lagged considerably behind practical requirements. Unable to find any support in theory, various methods of partial optimisation were used in practice. These were based on criteria such as the marginal rate of internal accumulation (or the projected rate of return) of a given investment variant, the pay-back period of capital outlays entailed by the choice of a more capital-intensive project, and so on.

The discussion on the theoretical foundations of economic calculations of investment efficiency in a centrally planned economy started in the Soviet Union. In its first phase (1946–54), there were four identifiable approaches. The first was associated with the practice in investment design bureaux which applied 'investment profitability norms', set arbitrarily by the central economic authorities, and similar yardsticks for calculating the return on investments. It was proposed to refine these norms and base the methods used on investment efficiency calculations on some universal standard such as the average rate of return. A second view was put forward primarily by S. Strumilin. He proposed basing efficiency calculations on the notion of depreciation payments for the use of productive equipment. He laid especial emphasis on allowing for the time factor in the calculation. Then there were various partial standards of investment efficiency that were widely used in Soviet investment design bureaux, such as the profitability period, and the pay-back period. These too had many supporters and were advocated by, among others, A. Lurie. (It is worth noting that, as early as 1946, he had pointed out that in a socialist economy, the national economic plan tells us *what* to produce, and investment efficiency calculation tells us only *how* to produce it. In his opinion, the latter ought to secure the conditions for maximising the growth of labour productivity in every industry and hence in the economy as a whole.) Finally there were the advocates of a macro-economic approach to investment efficiency appraisal, who pointed to the necessity for comprehensive research on the effects of investment activity on various aspects of social and economic life.

In Poland, it was these last two approaches that won most support. In 1955–6 Bronisław Minc and Kazimierz Secomski advocated the macro-economic approach to investment efficiency theory. Józef Pajestka and Mieczysław Rakowski, although working within the framework of the fourth approach, were more inclined towards practical applications, and in this sense were closer to the third approach. Kalecki became involved in these discussions in the autumn of 1956, when the Planning Commission set up a special team under his direction to work on improvements to the draft economic plan for 1956–60.[1] Among the achievements of this group was a thorough examination of about thirty key investment projects in that plan. The results of this work were used to change the structure of investment outlays in the Five Year Plan in order to increase their effectiveness (for example, in coal mining), or mitigate the consequences of reduced investment which, although it increased current consumption, could have slowed the pace of economic development. Increasing the efficiency of investment, which was the main aim of Kalecki's team, was one of the ways of eliminating the tendency for investment to squeeze current consumption.

From 1957 to 1959, Kalecki spoke at a number of meetings of the Planning Commission's Board about the efficiency of various investment projects in the 1956–60 and 1961–5 Five Year Plans.[2] However, he himself did little systematic work at that time on the methodological foundations of investment efficiency calculations, except for supervising the research conducted, mainly by Mieczysław Rakowski in the Economic Research Institute (*Zakład Badań Ekonomicznych*) of the Planning Commission. Between 1956 and 1959 a large number of analyses of the economic effectiveness of investment projects in various industries was completed. This provided the basis for testing and revising the calculus used up to that time. Kalecki undertook this latter task when he took charge of the Methodology Section of the Second Consultative Conference on Investment Efficiency Analysis (*II Krajowa Narada w Sprawie Badania Efektywności Inwestycji*). It was while he was working in this section that Kalecki and Rakowski prepared a new and radically different set of rules for calculating the efficiency of investment.

KALECKI AND RAKOWSKI'S NEW METHODOLOGY

The chief aim of economic efficiency calculation in the proposed new regulations was to enable a rational choice to be made between different investment projects, of which the more capital-intensive one has lower operating costs compared to the other projects. The basic difference between the new proposals and practice up to that time was that, in addition to the productive effects promised by alternative investment projects, account was now to be taken of their respective resource and foreign currency savings, under various capacity utilisation assumptions. The proposals were also made with the benefit of the results obtained from the second phase of Soviet discussions on investment efficiency.[3] However, these proposals were primarily intended to include in future calculations issues such as the tying-up of investment outlays in the course of construction, differences in the durability of alternative projects, differences in the time profile of output and costs, and the objective definition of a discount rate for investment.

This last issue and the marginal pay-back period, advocated in the new proposals, inspired much debate. Many argued in favour of discounting the value of production and costs at the same rate as that of average economic growth, in accordance with the 'Golden Rule' for accumulation. However, Kalecki felt that in a socialist economy with a commitment to permanent full employment, this method had no theoretical justification.

> This method is appropriate to a profit-maximising capitalist enterprise comparing the profitability of investment in fixed capital with investment in bonds offering a constant rate of return to find the most profitable solution. It is possible to imagine a socialist economy in which a discount method could be used. This would be an economy with unlimited labour reserves, whose aim would be the maximisation of accumulation. In reality, however, we assume that full employment exists in a socialist economy whose aim is the maximisation of national income.[4]

The main weakness of discounting in accordance with the 'Golden Rule' in a socialist economy is that it isolates the problem of the effectiveness of reducing operating costs by increasing investment outlays (implied in the choice of a more capital intensive variant) from the balance in the labour market. Should not the supply of labour have a bearing on the discount rate used in the selection of investment projects? For a given rate of capital accumulation, should the same discount rate apply regardless of the growth of labour supply? For Kalecki the answers were firmly in the negative. The discount rate (that is, the marginal pay-back period) was supposed to be determined in an iterative process, in which planned investment outlays in a given period were to match the available labour by selecting suitably capital-intensive (and hence labour-saving) new investment projects that qualify under each given rate of discount. (This differs from the standard approach to the 'choice of techniques' problem mainly in that the latter assumes the rate of interest to be given and postulates downward flexibility of wages, so that changing labout costs would maintain full employment in production.)

The proposed way of introducing the construction period into the calculation consisted of increasing investment outlays in proportion to the length of the construction period, and in inverse proportion to the capital intensity and labour cost intensity of producing a unit of national income, given the rate of discount, the scrapping rate of obsolete capacity, and the standard life-span of fixed capital.[5] The new formula allowed for a longer than standard life-span of capital and was adjusted to take into account variations in the time patterns of inputs and outputs. Despite these modifications and improvements, Kalecki and Rakowski considered the new solution to be 'no more than a better approximation to the complex economic reality than those now in use, rather than a final solution to the problem'.[6]

Further work and discussions led to the drawing up in the Planning Commission of a new General Instruction on the Methodology of Analyses of the Economic Efficiency of Investment (*Instrukcja ogólna w sprawie metodyki badán ekonomicznej efektywności inwestycji*: Warsaw, 1960), by Kalecki and Rakowski. The new instruction provided more thorough methodological foundations for such calculations, primarily in the following respects.

(1) The criteria for assessing the effectiveness of particular projects were more precisely linked to the general problems of extended reproduction, and especially the maximisation of national income with given material and labour resources.
(2) In analysing particular investment projects, allowance was made for variations in their subsequent conditions of operation and their economic environment.
(3) The general methods of analysing efficiency were modified and

adapted to particular activities such as international trade and co-operation, the extension and modernisation of existing industrial capacity and agriculture.

(4) Attempts were made to apply input–output analysis and linear programming in the analysis of infrastructural investments, the optimum conditions for industrial co-ordination between plant of widely differing economic characteristics, and so on.

(5) Studies of investment efficiency in the development of whole industries and economic sectors over longer-term periods of time were undertaken.[7]

This work revealed even more clearly the complexity of the methodological and accounting problems involved in analysing investment efficiency and showed that sometimes these even precluded altogether an unambiguous solution. This was because the effectiveness of actual investment undertakings is always tied up with future economic conditions which cannot be forecast precisely. There are also difficulties in summarising economic relationships in any regular function.

These difficulties are well illustrated in bringing into the calculation the production period of industrial plant. The method proposed by Kalecki and Rakowski in 1959, and promulgated subsequently in the 1960 General Instruction, was original and ingenious. Their solution seemed theoretically appropriate to the centrally planned economy with full-employment. However, it also inspired many doubts, and not just because of misapprehensions about it. The Kalecki and Rakowski method encouraged investment outlays that merely lengthened capacity life-span. This seemed incomprehensible when, arguably, these resources could have brought greater benefits in other applications.[8] The authors themselves were unaware that, given the values of the variables concerned, the investment efficiency formula gives a minimum only for a given production life-span. Only later, following further discussion, was the formula modified to remove this discrepancy.[9]

Many of these misapprehensions and disputes could probably have been avoided if it had been realised that, in the final analysis, there was not just one issue, but two. Having rejected the 'Golden Rule' discount method, Kalecki and Rakowski rightly concentrated attention on the problem of setting a discount rate (or a target pay-back period). But regardless of this, there is the problem of the accounting method used to make the inputs and outputs of various production processes commensurable after the discount rate has been fixed in some way or another. Thus, with different production life-spans and investment outlays, and outputs that vary over time and between each alternative method of production, the discounting is methodologically superior (it is recommended not just in welfare economics textbooks, but also by L. V. Kantorovich, V. V. Novozhilov and others). It is also simpler than successive versions of the Kalecki and Rakowski appraisal method.

Kalecki's work on the problem of measuring the effectiveness of modernisation and industrial development programmes was a further advance in making investment efficiency calculations more versatile. This was brought about by the need to obtain criteria for assessing the effectiveness of long-term programmes of investment in different sectors of the economy. Moreover, Kalecki was still in charge of various Planning Commission studies of investment and foreign trade efficiency. The outcome of these activities was the drawing up in 1962 of draft regulations on methods of appraising the economic efficiency of investment. This draft completed and expanded (especially in the area of modernisation and small-scale investment) the *General Instruction* in force since 1960. One of the aims of the new draft regulations was to induce investing enterprises to undertake more modernisation schemes, reducing the preference for capital-intensive works and thereby saving on investment resources.

The issuing of the new instructions for investment appraisal was accompanied by the publication of a revised and extended set of studies in the theory and practice of investment efficiency calculations. This book can be regarded as a summary of the work on investment efficiency appraisal carried out under Kalecki's direction in the Planning Commission. How practical were these studies, and was it possible to use them to obtain the same output at a significantly lower input cost? In his introduction to the book, Kalecki answered this question as follows:

> This depends entirely on setting out many different variants for each investment task. If this is not done, then the application of the theory becomes a barren exercise, since there is no problem of choice where there is only one project, or the problem is not very important if all the projects are fairly similar. The examples given in the book allow us to say that investment efficiency calculations can only secure significant savings if completely different variants of production are taken into account.[10]

The formulae for calculating investment efficiency contained in the *Instructions* of 1960 and 1962 were not the only ones in Polish economic literature at the time. In 1961, Bronisław Minc proposed a so-called 'annual outlay' (*nakładolat*, that is, the sum of total annual investment and operating costs in a given production process) method.[11] This method encouraged longer-lasting investments, and took no account of losses due to the perhaps longer than optimal production life-span. It also ignored the possibility of substitution between labour and investment outlays, which was precisely the key element in Kalecki's approach. However, in contrast to Kalecki, who sought a criterion of 'relative efficiency' which would enable a rational choice to be made between alternative investment projects, Minc set out to provide some 'absolute' measure of efficiency for any project.

Henryk Fiszel also put forward a method based on a rate of interest, discounting the streams of inputs and outputs for each investment project.[12] While it left unresolved the problem of how to set the discount rate, its accounting technique was more consistent than the method recommended in the Planning Commission's instructions. But apart from this, Fiszel's approach and that of the 1962 Instruction were the same.

Similar investment selection criteria were used in the other CMEA countries in the 1960s. Regulations about choosing between investment variants were usually based on the methods used in the Soviet Union. Only in Poland and Hungary did regulations depart significantly from Soviet model calculations in, for example, introducing a uniform marginal pay-back period and target rate of return, in place of pay-back periods differentiated by industry.

This convergence of the methods used in comparing the economic efficiency of investment created the opportunity to use them as a foundation for the international division of labour among socialist countries. Kalecki intended to use the results of such calculations, carried out according to their respective methodologies in each of the CMEA countries, as a step towards the co-ordination of perspective plans for economic development in these countries. He argued for this at many meetings of the Economic Commission of the CMEA from the autumn of 1959 onwards (see above pp. 73–7). But, after the initial discussions this initiative got bogged down in serious difficulties. In the first place, the working party set up to look at the issue came to the conclusion that fundamental theoretical research on the methodology of investment efficiency calculation should first be conducted. Only after having arrived at a uniform methodology, should it be applied in international comparisons of various specific investment undertakings.

Kalecki regarded this approach as mistaken. Instead he put forward a compromise solution under which the Soviet methodology and the standard pay-back periods proposed by the Soviet delegation should be provisionally accepted (indicating that the methodology used in some countries differed from the Soviet one). He feared that attempts to achieve theoretical consistency and uniformity between countries would lead to a protracted academic discussion about subjects on which there were significant differences of opinion, not only among individual countries but within them as well, notably in the Soviet Union. The Economic Commission of the CMEA did not seem to him to be the right forum for such a discussion. Moreover, it would have delayed work on the actual international comparisons that were the underlying purpose of the whole enterprise, and the basis of the long-term programme of specialisation.[13]

Nevertheless, Kalecki was well aware of the limitations of the application of investment efficiency calculations in determining the international labour division among the CMEA countries. He believed, for instance, that it could be used for the intra-industry rather than inter-industry specialisation.

> The use of comparisons of investment efficiency between different countries can be expected to have limited significance. This is immediately apparent if only from the fact that were a country to have a lower investment efficiency in all activities, its development would still not be stopped.
>
> As an example, a comparison of efficiency in constructing power stations was worked out. This showed a low efficiency in East Germany, a high one in Czechoslovakia, with that in Poland and the USSR occupying intermediate positions. Even without considering the weaknesses in the calculation, . . . it is impossible to draw any conclusion from it. For example, it can not be argued that East Germany should cease building power stations based on lignite, and import electricity from abroad. It is therefore undesirable to prejudge the use to be made of investment efficiency indicators.[14]

At the same time Kalecki urged that the overall balance of trade of the countries participating in the division of labour and the intra-industry specialisation should not be altered. In essence, he tried to base the co-operation of the CMEA countries on the co-ordination of their perspective development plans, drawn up on the basis of each country's own assessment of its needs and using the criteria that its government judged to be appropriate. However, as we have already mentioned, these efforts brought results that were far below his expectations.

Kalecki's contribution to the theory of investment efficiency appraisal consisted at this stage not only in proposing original solutions, but also in breaking through some established conventions of thought in Poland and other CMEA countries. But his approach was not without its own weak points. Perhaps the most important of these, which was not removed in subsequent years, and which it shared with the other calculation methods proposed at that time, was its insufficient comprehensiveness. With the current state of economic knowledge and techniques of calculation, it was impossible to perform a calculation which would account for all interdependencies throughout the economy. That is why the calculation stopped at partial optimisation which, it was believed, approached an overall economic optimum, and which was undoubtedly an improvement on using hardly any calculation at all. There was also the problem of the reliability of the information necessary to calculate the efficiency indicator of each investment project and, associated with the estimation of projected costs, the problem of devising a sufficiently large number of alternative projects. Then there was the problem of a faulty price structure underlying all these calculations, and so on. All these considerations suggested that the results of these calculations should be viewed with a degree of scepticism.

After leaving the Planning Commission in 1964, Kalecki's work on the theory of investment efficiency calculations was increasingly loosely linked to current needs for drawing up new regulations and instructions on the practical choice of investment variants. He was more attracted towards theoretical issues, such as the basis for optimising different variants of the structure of consumption, the link between investment efficiency calculations and growth theory, and improved methods of accounting for differences in the distribution over time of inputs and outputs in alternative investment variants.

PROBLEMS OF OPTIMISING THE STRUCTURE OF CONSUMPTION

According to Kalecki there are only three purposes to which economic efficiency calculations can be applied:

(1) the choice of the most economic method of realising a given production task;
(2) the choice of the right export or import-substituting investment; and
(3) securing the right structure of consumption.

This last was very difficult and required, *inter alia*, a knowledge of the price and income elasticities of demand for particular consumption goods. Under pressure to provide quickly practical guidelines, Kalecki initially concentrated on the methodology of choice of production processes for a given product, and foreign trade investments. Only when approximate solutions were found did he turn to the choice of consumption structure.

He was also prompted to more systematic work on this by the discussion on the 1961–5 Five Year Plan, and the 1961–75 Perspective Plan. The proposals for optimising the structure of national income put forward during these discussions did not always assume any defined composition of consumption. However, if this portion of national income were to undergo optimisation, with its volume expressed in constant prices (of the plan's first year, for example), then such a procedure could lead to absurd results. For example, if the most profitable (that is, having the highest ratio of consumption to outlay) item under the given price structure were to be, say, razor blades, then an 'optimal' composition of consumption would be one containing only razor blades.

The source of this paradox lies in the faulty definition of equivalence among various consumption variants, based on their comparative value expressed according to a fixed structure of prices. Let us suppose we have two bundles of consumer goods, clearly differing in their contents, but having the same value expressed in prices of the base period. Let us further suppose that only one of these bundles reflects actual consumption in that period. If in the following year the first bundle is replaced by the second bundle, and the price mechanism operates to equate supply with demand, then the realised value of the second bundle will almost certainly be different from that of the first bundle. This is because of the changed structure of supply. But if the value of the first bundle is calculated at the market clearing prices of the second bundle, then, in general, the two bundles will not be equivalent. What therefore should be accepted as the criterion for comparing different bundles of consumption?

It is apparent that, in fact, Kalecki faced the problem of what methodology ought to be used as the basis for a concept akin to the notion of the consumer's 'indifference curve', although his concept was to be used in a different context. Clearly here too it concerned an economy in which consumers select an optimum structure of consumption through market mechanisms. But Kalecki was addressing the central planner, whose macro-economic allocation of resources defines the supplied composition of consumer articles in the future.

In the indifference curve concept the consumers' optimising behaviour determines the equivalence of consumer bundles which therefore may be very different in their composition. From consumers' choices there follows an equality of the price ratios and the marginal quantity ratios, $dx/dy = -dp_x/dp_y$, in the standard notation. On the other hand, in Kalecki's concept of the 'curve of equivalent consumption bundles' it is the central planner who decides on the equivalence of different bundles, and it is the equality of the price ratios and the quantity ratios which makes them equivalent. (Both these concepts are implicitly linked to the Labour Theory of Value, according to which in equilibrium market clearing prices are equal to 'prices of production'.) To satisfy this condition of equivalence Kalecki needed there to be only minor and counterbalancing differences in the composition of the bundles compared; that is, an increase in the amount of one good would be accompanied by a decrease in the amount of another. Keeping all the time to the principle of making small and counterbalancing changes across the whole range of the goods (which justified neglecting as insignificant changes in relative prices resulting from alterations in the composition of the bundles) Kalecki obtained a chain of equivalent consumption structures. The curve thereby derived was concave.

Kalecki's subsequent argument did not depart significantly from that of the traditional Welfare Economics.[15] Among the equivalent bundles of consumer goods, the one with the lowest input cost is the one whose relative market clearing prices are equal to its relative costs of production. Kalecki calculated the costs of production as the total sum of unit capital costs and operating costs, using here the simplified formula for calculating the efficiency of investment.

Both the Welfare Economics approach and Kalecki's approach suffer from well-known weaknesses: the first because of the subjective character of the individual consumer's assessment, which can only be known *post factum*, and whose *ex ante* aggregation is neither possible nor, in a *laissez-faire* economy, is it at all necessary; the second because the central planner does not observe the restrictions necessary to arrange the different consumption bundles into a continuum, and does not take into account consumer preferences (that is, if any theory can be held responsible for failing to secure the correct behaviour on the part of the central authorities!). There are also the difficulties of discovering and then aggregating the *ex ante* individual preferences of consumers by the central planner, who needs them to determine the allocation of resources capable of producing in the future the 'optimum' consumption bundle.

However, the solution proposed by Kalecki has also an additional weakness, which also applies to his ideas on the choice of alternative investment projects, to which we shall return later. His approach does indeed take into account the interdependencies between the composition of consumer output and market prices, but there is a third variable which interacts with the other two. This is the rate of interest (conceptually equivalent here to the rate of discount or the marginal pay-back period used in the calculation of investment efficiency). In Kalecki's argument, the starting point is the rate of interest that has been set, and which influences long-run costs (that also appear in the investment efficiency indicators). With these costs, one arrives at a structure of production in which (taking into account the price elasticity of demand) price ratios are equal to long-term cost ratios. There is therefore a definite procedure followed through.

But here too there are doubts. The level of the rate of interest itself depends on the composition of final output that is to be produced. But we must choose this rate in advance, since without it we cannot determine long-term costs. Only subsequently can we find that structure of production whose price ratios are equal to its cost ratios. But the composition of production thereby arrived at may be different from that used to determine the rate of interest. In other words, there may be a different rate of interest appropriate to the final composition of output. If so, then the long-term cost ratios need to be changed and a new structure of production with its corresponding price ratios must be sought. It is not possible to be sure that repeating this procedure would bring us closer to a solution; that is, that this iterative process is convergent. On the contrary, the capital theory debates suggest that even small changes in the structure of production can give rise to very large changes in interest rates and prices and *vice versa*, and that monotonic changes in interest rates may be associated with non-monotonic changes in price ratios.[16] In the light of these debates, convergence does not seem to be a likely possibility.

The extent of the practical significance of this problem is unclear. Kalecki's approach would suggest that it is not significant. However, it is not apparent whether he ever reflected on precisely this issue, although he wrote in 1963 of the need to resolve many issues before computers can choose for us the best consumption variant.[17]

FURTHER DEVELOPMENTS OF KALECKI AND RAKOWSKI'S METHODOLOGY

The solution put forward by Kalecki and Rakowski at the beginning of the 1960s was implicitly based on the notion of an isoquant of production, representing different technological variants for obtaining a unit of national income of a given composition (with inputs and outputs expressed at some constant prices). This was the idea put forward by Kalecki in his *Introduction to the Theory of Growth in a Socialist Economy*, in which it was the basis of a taxonomy of technical progress and an analysis of the possibilities and consequences of accelerating economic growth through substituting embodied labour for living labour. However, this still gave rise to certain doubts.

A unit of national output consists of many items of final production. Usually each one can be produced using more than one method. The number of variants for producing a unit of national income can therefore be very large (with n items of final output, and only two methods of producing each one of them, there will be 2^n variants for producing a unit of final output). Some of these variants will be absolutely inefficient; that is, with the same outlay, more of at least one item of production could be produced. Since the central planner is not in a position to examine all the variants to eliminate those that are absolutely inefficient, it could be argued that the production curve is a purely theoretical construct: in practice all the points along the curve may not be available, and therefore the possibility of selecting an absolutely inefficient variant for producing an increment in national output cannot be excluded.

In his later work, Kalecki showed that an efficient variant for producing an increment of national output can in fact be arrived at. This could happen if the investment efficiency calculation is used at intermediate management levels to select a production method for each item (or items) of final output. Then for each rate of interest (discounting future inputs and outputs), there would correspond a definite point on the production curve. If we assume that labour is homogeneous, that there is only one rate of interest, and the productive life-span of each method of production is the same, then it can be shown that the production curve will be concave.

The selection methods actually used in the socialist countries in the 1960s were in fact less rigorous, and they also allowed for:

(a) varying labour outlays giving rise to changes in the average wage;
(b) interest rate differentiation according to the branch of production; and
(c) varying productive life-spans for different equipment.

In this case, it is no longer possible to show that the production curve is concave, but merely that it is downward-sloping. Nevetheless, Kalecki still thought that actual production curves could probably be satisfactorily approximated by concave curves. In these, for a given labour outlay there would correspond some minimum investment outlay necessary to produce an increase in national income of a given size and composition.[18]

The concept of the production curve enables us to determine the rate of interest that corresponds to the planned increase in national income, and the increase in employment required to obtain it. In fact, if we draw the production curve for the target increase in national income, we can identify the point on it that corresponds to the amount of available labour. This then gives us the investment outlay required, while the slope of the curve at that point gives us the rate of interest (the standard pay-back period) which needs to be applied in investment efficiency calculations in order to arrive at that point, and thus to ensure equilibrium in the labour market.[19]

It should be pointed out that accelerations in the economic growth rate through additional mechanisation, analysed in greater detail in Kalecki's theory of growth, are effected through changes in the rate of interest in investment efficiency calculations. These in turn induce the choice of more capital-intensive methods of production; that is, selecting a new point on the given production curve. This mechanism is thus analogous to the free market mechanism in neo-classical economics. In this way the production curve links up the theory of investment efficiency with the theory of growth in a socialist economy.

In Kalecki's analysis, each point on the production curve represents the productive effect of new investments, without deducting the effects of the retirement of old equipment. Hence, the supply of labour corresponding to it includes not just its natural increase, but also the labour made redundant due to the elimination of out-of-date equipment. In other words, each point on the production curve represents an actual variant of gross new investment. In 1967 Rakowski tried to modify this analysis, seeking to break gross investment down into replacement and net investment. He wanted each point on the production curve to correspond to some combination of retired worn-out equipment, its replacement, and investment in new plant. Kalecki considered this to be a very valuable contribution. This approach allowed a clear demonstration that any modification to old productive apparatus, by contrast with new plant, is unrepeatable. (This is why, for example, a given modernisation of equipment, resulting in a defined increase in production, cannot ultimately be regarded as one variant: It cannot be repeated at will or on any desired scale in order to achieve the required increase in production.) Kalecki's subsequent researches went in the direction of such reconstructions of the production curve.[20]

As in earlier formulations, the substance of the investment efficiency calculation consisted of achieving an increase in national income of a given magnitude and composition, using the smallest possible outlay on investment, but which would nevertheless maintain full employment throughout the period in question. Standard rates of discount were kept, fulfilling a balancing function in the iterative process of equalising the demand for additional labour with its supply. The problem consisted in showing that the new formula for calculating investment efficiency does not alter the fundamental properties of the production curve. The new formula allowed for differences in the growth rate between different industries (but remaining constant over the time horizon of the analysis), and took into account the retirement of old equipment and its modernisation. In other words, the problem was to see if a downard-sloping, concave production curve would still give a good summary, under more realistic conditions, of the efficient variants for producing a given increase in national income.

The central dilemma was therefore to show that the criterion for minimising inputs, expanded to include these conditions in the formula, would still lead to the selection of a minimum input variant. Kalecki showed that it would, and that the methodology of the calculation (which remained unchanged from the original Kalecki and Rakowski version in the early 1960s) was still correct. Moreover, he showed that it was not only correct under the conditions described above, but also when the formula is adapted to take account of different raw materials usage in different variants, technical progress, and when choices over the composition of foreign trade are introduced. He also showed that, using this formula, the iterative process of balancing investment outlays with the available labour supply would probably be convergent.[21]

However, in selecting technological variants and the composition of foreign trade, there remains one problem unresolved by Kalecki. This is the interdependence between the technological solution (or the structure of foreign trade) chosen, prices, and the rate of interest at which inputs and outputs are calculated. What do the constant prices used for aggregation, which are not adjusted each time there is a change in the structure of inputs, outputs and the rate of interest, actually represent? Is not too high a price paid for the convergence of iterative processes, for which such inflexible prices are a necessary, but insufficient, condition, since they may cease to reflect production costs?[22] We can offer no satisfactory answer to these questions.

CHANGES IN THE CRITERIA OF CALCULATION DURING THE 1970s: CAUSES AND CONSEQUENCES

At the end of the 1960s, partly in association with the discussion in the European socialist countries about various proposed economic reforms, considerable criticism was made of the criteria for assessing investment efficiency. These criteria required comparisons of combined unit costs, expressed in natural units. However, this was at variance with the principle of conducting each calculation in value terms only. Moreover, the different criteria used in calculating efficiency during the investment phase and during the subsequent production phase meant that economic calculation in one phase was separated from economic calculation in the second phase.

New appraisal principles for investment projects were first introduced in Czechoslovakia in 1967. The methodology used up to that time, based on Soviet models, was replaced by calculations based on discounted streams of inputs and outputs in the whole production process, starting from investment outlays right up to plant retirement. In Poland, the first changes were introduced in 1969. These covered calculations of investment efficiency not just for the choice of production methods but also in the, albeit limited, field of decisions concerning the composition of production in the enterprise.[23] Similar changes in the practice of investment efficiency calculation were introduced in the USSR.[24]

Kalecki was decidedly against such an extension of the scope of investment efficiency calculations. He considered that, in a socialist economy, it was only methodologically appropriate to calculate the relative efficiency of substituting the factors of production needed to produce *a given use-value*. Therefore he was against replacing this type of calculation with a micro economic calculation of absolute efficiency whose rationale is exchange value. In his opinion, it was primarily the plan which should decide the choice of size and composition of use value.

Let us suppose that we have a closed economy in which there is only one production technology for each use-value, and in which the central planner determines unambiguously in a long-term plan the growth path of national income (measured in constant prices), the structure of consumption and non-productive investment, and their relative dimensions in each year of the plan. In this economy, there exists only one balanced variant of the plan and, according to Kalecki, the problem of calculating investment efficiency does not arise at all. Only with the possibility of choosing production techniques, and varying the composition of foreign trade, do we get two degrees of freedom:

> It is within the framework of these degrees that the evaluation of investment efficiency can operate – given the assumptions made by the planning authorities about the growth rate of national income, the structure of consumption and unproductive investment.[25]

The investment efficiency calculation can be extended to include the choice of the 'cheapest' consumption structure. However, this requires the introduction of a criterion of equivalence for various consumption aggregates. Neither Kalecki's initial idea for this, nor his method for selecting the structure of consumption in the perspective plan were developed in subsequent years. He therefore recommended that decisions regarding the structure of consumption (together with unproductive investment) should be treated as exogenous in the different plan variants corresponding to different growth rates: 'In such conditions, the field in which we assess the efficiency of investment is . . . the choice of techniques for the achievement of given production targets and the pattern of exports and imports'.[26]

Kalecki's view did not prevail. The new principles of investment efficiency appraisal, introduced in Poland in 1975, were based on discounting streams of future costs and revenues. They linked investment efficiency with the financial system of the enterprise through the repayment (with depreciation, in principle) of investment credits and through the interest paid on credit outstanding.[27] The purpose of the new rule was to standardise and improve methods of calculating investment efficiency, and to link them up with efficiency appraisals of current production and the financial systems of enterprises. The enterprise director was supposed to be responsible for the economic performance of the enterprise, contingent upon proper economic calculation. (In practice, this responsibility turned out to be illusory.)

The new rules aroused several reservations, especially with respect to the method of determining the investment efficiency norm (the standard rate of interest).[28] In accordance with Kalecki's approach, the marginal pay-back period used in Poland in investment regulations from the beginning of the 1960s was a macro-economic variable. It was set in the course of regulating the balance in the labour market in a given period, while minimising investment outlays in the economy as a whole. In the *Outline Instruction* of 1975 the target rate of efficiency was made equal to the rate of interest then applied by the central bank to the credits that it granted. However, it was not obvious why it was exactly this target rate of investment efficiency, and what instrument were to be used in conjunction with it in order to balance resources which had previously been balanced by setting an appropriate marginal pay-back period. At the roots of these doubts lay a much more fundamental difference between the two approaches to investment efficiency calculations.

Kalecki sought to give economic calculation under socialism a social dimension. In his view, the rationale for socialism was that different criteria of social rationality should be used in economic decision-making from those used under the capitalist system. In particular, sectional interests should be subject to the overall social interest, defined by the central planner. On this basis, Kalecki gave prominence to use-value in economic calculation under socialism. The aim, according to him, was to maximise the volume of a given structure of national income rather than its exchange value.

The instructions introduced in the 1970s led to quasi-market solutions and sought to eliminate overall social considerations, like the marginal pay-back period, from efficiency calculations. In place of maximising a national income of a given structure, the aim became to maximise its exchange value. The changes aimed at adapting market mechanisms in such a way that the market mechanism, and not the central planner, ultimately decides the structure of production. These attempts were partly inspired by a belief that as long as investment appraisal calculations merely determine relative (and not absolute) efficiency, it is impossible to break away from an administrative/rationing system of economic management.

Market prices, which in the new system were to function as objective criteria for efficiency assessments, are in fact only *relatively* objective indicators of social production costs under competitive market conditions. Meanwhile, the prices used in investment efficiency appraisals in Poland during the 1970s, like the other parameters of this calculation, were manipulated and distorted according to the preferences of the central authorities and monopolistic industrial organisations. As a result, 'absolute' efficiency indicators were based on elastic but arbitrary prices (and rarely on world prices) and other changeable and manipulated parameters. The effect was to make investment efficiency calculation even more subjective than before.

An effective choice of investment variants requires the availability of at least two independent variants of each investment task. In the absence of competition, this then requires appropriate institutional arrangements to secure the drawing up of alternative plans, and to allow the choice of the variant that is best from the overall social, and not necessarily narrowly industrial, point of view. Kalecki laid great stress on this institutional requirement:

> I consider it necessary to create a central institution, employing suitably qualified engineers and economists, which would not only

> assess the investment projects submitted to it, but also put forward counter-proposals. It seems that this is the only way to bring about on a greater scale the use of the principle of analysing different variants. The activity of such an institution could also contribute to raising the standard of the preliminary checking of the projects submitted (independently of the analysis of their efficiency). Only working on the design of investment schemes, even if it is merely preliminary design analysis, can one obtain a feel for the basic data which, in the form of the project submitted, may not be strictly accurate, to put it mildly.[29]

The main weakness of this proposal results from its somewhat academic character. It implies a mechanism for preparing and making investment decisions in a socialist economy, in which investors are directed by the general social interest, and not primarily by their own particular interests. In practice, however, sectional points of view prevailed, manifesting themselves in pressures to apply the most modern and highly automated techniques of production, without regard for financial and social costs and the possibilities of adapting these techniques to conditions of production. Investors were primarily interested in securing for themselves the greatest possible resources, since bonuses, rewards and other material incentives for management and workforce depended on the size of their investment commitments. These interests gave rise to the phenomenon of 'getting into the plan' favoured projects by lowering costs and/or exaggerating their benefits, knowing that withdrawal from already started schemes is always costly and done with reluctance by the central planner.

Kalecki's proposal threatened these particular industrial interests. Hence their strong opposition to it. There was also opposition from the central economic authorities, since it would subject their decisions too to more rigorous accounting. This explains the subsequent institutional reorganisation, which went counter to Kalecki's advice. In fact, decisions concerning new investments were not handed over to enterprises, but were left with the central planner. Instead of creating a central institution to work out alternative schemes for major investments, it was decided in 1969 to close the Planning Commission's *Biuro Ekspertów dla Oceny Projektów Inwestycyjnych* (Bureau for the Assessment of Investment Projects). Thus in the 1970s, at the time of the greatest post-war investment boom in Poland, there was no institution which could examine the social profitability of various investment projects. Reservations notwithstanding, applying Kalecki's method of investment appraisal would have helped to avoid many mistaken investment decision that were made during these years, if only industrial interests and the arbitrariness of the central authorities could have been overcome.

The substance and the institutional foundations of investment efficiency calculations are closely interlinked with the system of economic management. In fact, the latter largely determines which of the two basic options may be followed in the field of investment efficiency appraisal. The first option relates to a system of management in which investment decisions (except in armaments, infrastructure, health, education and similar services, regional development, and the like) are made at the enterprise level. Indeed, it may be argued that the arbitrary character of investment decision-making in Poland could not be limited mainly because further constraints were placed on enterprise autonomy – while constant assurances about its extension were purely rhetorical. Therefore the experience of the 1970s does not disprove the proposition that what, how and on what scale to produce, and the pattern of investment, should be decided by autonomous, self-managing enterprises. Market prices and other parameters of economic calculation – partially centrally regulated – would then carry out those functions which they had not been able hitherto to perform.

In the field of investment, this system is obviously consistent with the approach to efficiency appraisal started at the beginning of the 1970s, Decision-making is in this case left to the enterprise, and the function of market mechanisms is to control it. This solution has many well-known advantages over the administrative/rationing system. However, it has two fundamental weaknesses. First of all, without well-developed market mechanisms, ensuring that consumers get their preferred amount and composition of final output, leaving production and investment decisions to enterprises must lead to a situation in which they may produce neither what the central planners want, nor what consumers would prefer. Using market imperfections, monopoly prices and so on, they will produce whatever best satisfies the particular interests of each enterprise. Secondly, even if we do have perfect competition (let us remember that for Kalecki this was always only a convenient simplifying assumption), then investment decision-making solely on the basis of market assessments leads to the replacement of criteria of macro-economic rationality by those of micro-economic rationality. The adverse consequences of this have been widely discussed in economic literature.

A second solution consists of leaving the central planner with all investment decisions, except for the choice of the investment variant for obtaining a given use-value. In this solution, Kalecki's suggestions about the scope and the form of investment efficiency calculations resume their significance. Macro-economic accounting criteria and use-values are used to maximise national output of a given composition. This has its advantages: the use of an economic calculation which maximises the use-value of national output, and not its exchange-value, has particular attractions in view of increasingly apparent constraints on natural resources. But it also has the well-known disadvantages of a system of economic management in which almost the whole weight of economic decision-making is located outside the enterprise. The latter is directed by plan instructions from higher levels of management, rather than by signals from its suppliers and customers. In addition, there are methodological problems with Kalecki's proposals. We have already mentioned the difficulty of obtaining convergence in an iterative process with aggregation prices changing with each change in the rate of interest (or the difficulties of using constant prices in comparing the outlays and output of particular investment variants). There is also the problem of integrating the calculation of investment efficiency with the calculation of efficiency in the operational phase, and so on. Clearly too, with a solution of this kind, there are further problems in providing the institutional foundations for generating genuine investment alternatives.

The way in which an economy functions, both in the case of innovation in the socialist enterprise and in the case of investment efficiency calculation, to a large extent defines its substance and organisational characteristics. This system of functioning in turn is an integral part of the institutional and structural basis of the whole socio-political system. In large measure, this basis defines the mechanisms and forms in which particular interests are reconciled with the general interest. The lack of success up to now in applying in practice a new wholly decentralised approach to investment efficiency calculation testifies to its incompatibility with these wider aspects of the present Polish social and political system. The old approach, however, does not seem compatible with the economic efficiency needed to overcome the present Polish economic and political crisis.

Notes

1. See above, p. 78.
2. See, for example, Minute no. 4 of the meeting of the Planning Commission Board on 14 January 1958, AKPRM 10/4 and AKPRM 10/12.
3. See C. Grabowski, 'Dyskusja nad zagadnieniami ekonomicznej efektywności inwestycji a Związku Radzieckim' ('The Discussion in the USSR on the Economic Efficiency of Investment') *Gospodarka Planowa* (1959), no. 1.
4. M. Kalecki, 'W sprawie metodologii badań efektywności inwestycji' ('On the Methodology of Analysing the Efficiency of Investment') *Inwestycje i Budownictwo* (1959), no. 11, pp. 9–10, reproduced in *Dzieła*, vol. IV, pp. 309–13. The method for calculating investment efficiency that was proposed by Kalecki was limited to the choice of methods of producing an incremental unit of national output, whose structure is fixed a priori. In particular therefore it did not allow for any changes in the relative shares of accumulation and consumption in national income. In these circumstances, maximising national income is equivalent to maximising consumption. Only in this context does Kalecki speak of maximising national income as the aim of economic policy under socialism. This cannot therefore be taken as meaning that Kalecki held the view that maximising national income rather than consumption was the purpose of socialist economic activity.
5. M. Kalecki and M. Rakowski, 'Generalised Formula of the Efficiency of Investment', in A. Nove and D. M. Nuti, *Socialist Economics* (Harmondsworth: Penguin, 1972).
6. Ibid. p. 262.
7. See Kalecki's introduction to M. Rakowski *Efektywność inwestycji* (*The Efficiency of Investment*) (Warsaw, 1961).
8. C Józefiak, 'O rachunku efektywności inwestycji polemicznie' ('Polemically about Investment Efficiency Calculation'), *Życie Gospodarcze* (1960) no. 44.
9. M. Rakowski, 'Okres eksploatacji w wzorze efektywności inwestycji' ('The Production Period in the Investment Efficiency Formula'), *Gospodarka Planowa* (1961), no. 10.
10. M. Kalecki, introduction to M. Rakowski, *Efektywność inwestycji*, and *Dzieła*, vol. IV, pp. 326–7.
11. B. Minc, 'Efektywność ekonomiczna inwestycji w gospodarce socjalistycznej' ('The Economic Efficiency of Investment in a Socialist Economy'), *Ekonomista* (1961), no. 10.
12. H. Fiszel, *Efektywność inwestycji a optimum produkcji w gospodarce socjalistycznej* (*The Efficiency of Investment and the Optimum Production in a Socialist Economy*) (Warsaw, 1963).
13. Report of the Polish Delegation to the VI Meeting of the CMEA Economic Commission in Warsaw on 19 and 20 December 1961, AKPRM 301/9. See also M. Kalecki, *Dzieła*, vol. IV, pp. 328–9.
14. M. Kalecki, *Dzieła*, vol. IV, pp. 330–1.
15. P. A. Samuelson, 'The Consumption Theory in Terms of Revealed

Preferences', *Economica* (1948). Kalecki's methodology is also analogous to D. G. Champernowne's chain index of capital, in the latter's 'The Production Function and the Theory of Capital: A Comment', *Review of Economic Studies* 1953–4), no. 2. See also J. Osiatyński, *Kapitał podział wartość: kryzys ekonomii neomarginalistycznej* (*Capital, Distribution and Value: The Crisis of Neo-marginalist Economics*) (Warsaw, 1978), pp. 141–5.

16. P. Garegnani, 'Heterogeneous Capital, the Production Function and the Theory of Distribution', *Review of Economic Studies* (1970), no. 3.
17. M. Kalecki, 'The Problem of the Optimum Structure of Consumption', *Mathematical Studies in Economics and Statistics in the USSR and Eastern Europe: A Journal of Translations* (1965), no. 4, pp. 3–16, and *Dzieła*, vol. IV, p. 17–4.
18. M. Kalecki, 'The Curve of Production and the Evaluation of the Efficiency of Investment in a Socialist Economy', in *Socialism, Capitalism and Economic Growth: Essays in Honour of Maurice Dobb* (Cambridge University Press, 1967). It should be noted that Kalecki's procedure for selecting investment variants excludes the possibility of a convex production curve (in which case it would represent absolutely inefficient variants). Therefore the production curve representing efficient variants can be either a straight downward-sloping curve, in which case we have a trivial solution (since only the variants represented by the points at each end of the curve are worth further consideration) or else the criterion is insufficient to enable a choice to be made. Alternatively it is a concave curve, and this is the case which Kalecki considered. Kalecki's production curve differs from the corresponding production function in neo-classical economics in that the former concerns the product-mix which constitutes an incremental unit of national output, and not one product only, and in that it is derived from the characteristics of the variants compared. Otherwise they both share similar advantages and similar problems.
19. Ibid.
20. M. Kalecki, 'Basic Problems in the Theory of the Efficiency of Investment', in *Selected Essays on the Economic Growth of the Socialist and the Mixed Economy* (Cambridge University Press, 1972).
21. At the same time Kalecki warned against 'convergence arising from the lack in many instances of fundamentally differing technical variants (this is a basic problem relating to the practical use of the theory of investment efficiency, which is a theory which cannot in itself *give rise* to new investment variants)', ibid., p. 143.
22. This is further discussed in J. Osiatyński, 'Efekty Wicksell'a a efektywność inwestycji' ('Wicksell Effects and the Efficiency of Investment'), *Ekonomista* (1975), no. 4.
23. See *Uchwała 103 Rady Ministrów z dnia 7 czerwca 1969r. w sprawie metod oceny i klasyfikowania nowo rozpoczynanych inwestycji przemysłowych w latach 1971–1975* (*Council of Ministers Resolution no. 103, dated 7 June 1969, on Appraisal Methods and the Classification of Newly Commenced Industrial Investments in 1971–1975*), and *Przepisy o*

planowaniu i inwestycjach (*Regulations on Planning and Investment*) (Warsaw, 1969).

24. See L. V. Kantorovich, V. N. Bogachev and V. L. Makarov, 'Ob otsenkie efiektivnosti kapitalnikh zatrat', *Ekonomika i Matematicheskiye Mietody* (1970), no. 6; and 'Mietodika opriedieleniya ekonomicheskoy efiektivnosti isplozovaniya v narodnom khoziastvie novoy tekhniki', *Ekonomicheskaya Gazieta* (1977), no. 10.
25. M. Kalecki, 'The Scope of the Evaluation of the Efficiency of Investment in a Socialist Economy', in *Selected Essays on the Economic Growth of the Socialist and the Mixed Economy*, p. 121.
26. Ibid., p. 122.
27. 'Ramowe wytyczne w sprawie metodyki oceny ekonomicznej efektywności inwestycji produkcyjnych zamierzeń z zakresu postępu technicznego, organizacyjnego, współpracy gospodarczej i naukowo-technicznej oraz zamierzeń, których realizacja opiera sie na licencjach zagranicznych' ('Outline Instructions on the Method for the Economic Appraisal of Productive Investment Proposals for Technical and Organisational Progress, Scientific Co-operation, and Proposals Entailing the Use of Foreign Licences'), *Inwestycje i Budownictwo* (1974), no. 9, and *Ocena ekonomiczna efektywności inwestycji i innych zamierzeń rozwojowych: Zbiór przepisów* (*The Economic Appraisal of the Efficiency of Investment and Other Development Proposals: Collected Instructions*) (Warsaw, 1974).
28. In addition to Kalecki, Rakowski assumed a critical attitude to the new regulations in his article 'O niektórych podstawowych problemach rozwoju rachunku efektywności inwestycji' ('On Some Fundamental Problems of the Development of Investment Efficiency Calculation'), *Gospodarka Planowa* (1972), no. 4. The new instructions were defended by J. Czarnek and P. Glikman, 'O nowe ujęcie metodyki rachunku ekonomicznej efektywnosci inwestycji' ('On the New Method for the Economic Appraisal of Investment Efficiency'), *Inwestycje i Budownictwo* (1972), no. 1.
29. M. Kalecki, 'Uwagi o planie gospodarczym na lata 1966–1970' ('Observations on the 1966–1970 Economic Plan'), *Życie Gospodarcze* (1964), no. 15, pp. 1–2 (reproduced in *Dzieła*, vol. III, pp. 285–97).

7 Some Social and Economic Problems of Post-War Poland

COMPARING POST-WAR AND PRE-WAR PERSONAL INCOMES

Kalecki was well aware of the connections between the assessments that particular classes and social groups make of their material living conditions, and systems of economic incentives and management, the growth of labour productivity, and so on. On his return to Poland he criticised the practice of raising piece-work rates in proportion to increased labour productivity specifically because it ignored these connections (see p. 20). He talked about this on various occasions during 1956 and 1957, explaining that improvements in the material conditions of the population were just as important as institutional and organisational changes in resolving the current socio-economic problems of Poland. In his essay on the basic principles of long-term planning, he openly stated that neglect of consumption in the short term can undermine society's awareness of the value of socialism.

But empirical work on the level and changes in living standards in post-War Poland also had another merit in Kalecki's eyes. He was an economist whose work was permeated through and through by the realities of economic life. He sought confirmation of the slogans and ideas of social transformation not in ideological and political declarations, and commemorative speeches by national leaders, but in actual per capita or per worker consumption indicators, and in social awareness of them. In fact he had already shown an interest in this during the 1930s in the Polish Research Institute for the Study of Economic Cycles and Prices (*Instytut Badań Koniunktur Gospodarczych i Cen*). Together with the eminent Polish economist and statistician Ludwik Landau, he worked out estimates of Polish national income in 1929 and 1933 which were unique in the world at that time in that they divided up the consumed part of income into the shares of particular social classes and strata.[1] The results of this work remain a valuable source of materials for the analysis of differences in the economic status of different population groups in Poland at two turning points of the business cycle: in 1929, when workers' consumption reached its maximum in terms of highest wages and lowest unemployment in the decade 1927–37, and in 1933, in the trough of the 1929–33 crisis.

These studies of the income levels of manual and white-collar workers in 1929 and 1933 were the starting point for Kalecki's analysis of the scale of higher income and structural changes in income distribution in Poland after 1945. His first studies on changes in workers' incomes between 1937 and 1954 were conducted at the end of 1955 as part of his advisory work for Hilary Minc. This enabled him to obtain a lot of information on a period whose data on the size and distribution of workers' incomes is particularly sparse. The studies themselves were not published until the early 1980s.

After estimating gross and net income per head of the working population (that is, of workers and their families) in 1937, based on estimates for 1929, Kalecki compared real net incomes in 1954 and 1937. These included welfare payments, insurance payments and pensions. The comparison revealed that the 20 per cent increase in the per capita incomes of the working population took place 'thanks to an increase in the rate of employment . . . Real net income per employee in fact did not increase, and probably even fell'.[2] The average gross income of an employee in manufacturing rose by only 2 per cent between 1937 and 1954. But the change in the average earnings of workers in general was much worse outside industry. He also showed that a rise in the earnings of manual workers in manufacturing industry was accompanied by a sharp fall in the earnings of white-collar workers.

In the 1960s, Kalecki undertook further studies of changes in the incomes of manual and white-collar workers in Poland. He showed that between 1960 and 1937 the standard of living of manual workers outside agriculture more than doubled, but there was a fall in that of white-collar workers.[3] However, income growth per employee was much less. Manual workers on average enjoyed incomes about 75 per cent higher in 1960 than in 1937. The average income of a white-collar employee fell by about 20 per cent. If domestic servants and craftsmen are excluded, then the increase for manual workers is reduced to 45 per cent. Thus the raising of living standards was obtained by much more modest increases in earnings for comparable work. There was also a considerable fall in income differentials between manual and white-collar workers. The latter, who in pre-war Poland belonged to the privileged classes, in 1960 earned on average little more than manual workers.

In the light of these results, Kalecki tried to explain differences in the way in which various social groups saw their incomes in comparison to their pre-war conditions. He pointed out that on the whole people compare their incomes with corresponding incomes before the Second World War without taking into account the elimination of either unemployment or very low paid work. Thus, if the popular perception of income changes was less favourable than the actual increase in living standards, this was in Kalecki's view for the following reasons:

> First of all, white-collar workers feel themselves to have been severely wronged. As for manual workers' incomes, these have appreciated greatly even if we take comparable work as a starting point. But this increase is considerably less than the very great increase in the average living standard of the working population. Moreover it should be borne in mind that
>
> (a) even among manual workers, the increase in income for the same work is rather small for those employed outside industry; and
> (b) among industrial workers, more skilled and experienced workers have gained less than younger, unskilled workers.[4]

Kalecki did not regard this kind of change in the incomes of non-agricultural workers and its influence on the outlook of the urban population as either transitory or specifically Polish. In his view these changes were characteristic of the development of socialist countries starting from a low level of economic development. In these countries, even a considerable increase in consumption is swallowed up in raising very low rural standards of living, the costs of the rural population's migration to better paid urban occupations and the elimination of unemployment and low-paid work in the urban economy (where the existence of a lumpenproletariat is a form of concealed unemployment). Thus only a small part of the overall increase in consumption can be allocated to raising real wage rates. Nevertheless, if in a country like Poland wage rates are increased, this is bound to be in part at least at the cost of a substantial fall in the real earnings of white-collar workers. Kalecki realised that the resulting popular perceptions and behaviour can cause serious difficulties during the socialist development of less developed countries. But he felt that such an incomes policy was 'the only possible pattern of economic development that was based on principles of social justice'.[5]

In 1965–7, under the auspices of the Polish Academy of Sciences Kalecki started studying the changes in the incomes of manual and white-collar workers that took place between 1956 and 1965. This was a continuation of his earlier research. He also intended to undertake an analysis of very high personal incomes, which were not usually included in statistical surveys. Using as a reference point external manifestations of wealth, he wanted to verify widely held views about the numbers of the wealthiest groups in Polish society. The first of these studies was broken off as a direct result of the events of 1968, and the second was not even started.

AGRICULTURAL DEVELOPMENT

In examining the problems of economic growth and long-term planning, Kalecki was deeply aware that the tendency for agricultural production to lag behind the growth of production generally, and the whole complex issue of food supply and agricultural development were key factors in economic development overall. At the end of 1955 he put forward a system of subsidies for agricultural producer co-operatives. The essential idea behind this was to provide state guarantees for a part of the income of these co-operatives. This was meant to provide an additional incentive to co-operative members to work on its behalf.[6]

Kalecki always opposed all dogmatic and facile analyses of the problem of Polish agricultural development. He argued in favour of expanding state support for agriculture based on long-term contracts with producers, and of developing various forms of co-operation among private farmers. The state contract system obviously did not establish socialist relations of production in agriculture. But Kalecki felt that its main deficiency was that it made farm incomes dependent on the respective acreages of farms, rather than that it sustained private ownership of farmland.

In Kalecki's view, agricultural associations, in which private farmers shared equipment and jointly purchased materials, were essential for agricultural development. But he felt that their concern with agricultural mechanisation was exaggerated. Such mechanisation could really only be effective in large-scale farming. As long as agriculture remained predominantly small-scale, agricultural associations should provide farmers with the services needed to expand production, and should contribute to the intensification of agriculture through better use of fertilisers and fodder, the promotion of more suitable crops, improved livestock, and other techniques adapted to small-scale farming. But he laid primary emphasis on the need to develop state farms and especially agricultural co-operatives. He was so much in favour of collective farms that he even opposed private plots for collective farm members, believing that they dissipated the co-operative movement in agriculture. However, the main factor that he thought would transform small-scale private agriculture into large-scale and efficient state and co-operative agriculture was to be not administrative compulsion, but the exceptionally long working day in private agriculture. As living standards rose, this would become increasingly anomalous (see also p. 67).

Kalecki also opposed the argument that the tendency for growth of labour productivity in agriculture to lag behind that of industry was an obstacle to the development of the socialist economy. In contrast to a capitalist economy, in which productivity growth is the aim of economic activity because it raises the profits of capitalists, in the socialist economy it is a means of increasing national income and per capita consumption. If, as in Poland at that time, the economic growth rate is constrained not by shortages of labour, but by the slow growth of its raw materials base, including agricultural production, then a more rapid increase in agricultural productivity could only contribute to reducing working hours in non-agricultural sectors of the economy (assuming that full employment is maintained). It would not directly contribute to raising production in those sectors. Kalecki therefore suggested that agricultural policy and planning should aim to maximise productivity per hectare, rather than productivity per worker.[7]

But, above all, Kalecki criticised the view that there was some simple solution to the problems of agricultural backwardness. He warned in particular against

> planning, on the basis of faith in the absolute efficacy of some single factor, a fantastic rate of growth and, as a result, getting an actual growth rate that was considerably lower than one that could have been achieved with realistic planning of agricultural development.[8]

ON ECONOMIC DELINQUENCY

At the start of the 1960s the view that economic delinquency was on the decline, due to the elimination of the conditions in which it flourished, was widely advanced in the Polish media. However, this contrasted with many obvious manifestations of the rise of a 'black market bourgeoisie'. The 'laundering' of illegal earnings and its effect on the distribution of income was all the more glaring in view of the remarkably small differences in legal incomes at that time between virtually all social groups: rural and urban dwellers, manual and white-collar workers, management and workers. Kalecki was inspired by these contrasts to analyse the problem of economic delinquency. He saw the struggle against it as not only a normal corrective in economic life, but also as a 'necessary part of the achievement of socialism'.[9]

The attempt to explain the causes of economic delinquency was conducted under the auspices of the Polish Academy of Sciences. A working group was set up under Kalecki's direction to study various aspects of this question. The materials were supplied by the representatives on the group of the *Najwyższa Izba Kontroli* (the Highest Chamber of Control, the body responsible in Poland for overseeing the proper conduct of public administration), the *Główny Inspektorat Kontrolno-Rewizyjny Ministerstwa Finansów* (the Chief Audit and Control Inspectorate of the Finance Ministry), and the *Instytut Handlu Wewnętrznego* (the Internal Trade Institute). At the request of the working group, the Internal Trade Institute conducted a survey of various corrupt practices in the retail trade. On the basis of this and other information, a report was drawn up entitled 'Eknomiczne i organizacyjne problemy przestępczości gospodarczej' ('Economic and Organisational Problems of Economic Delinquency'). It was hoped that the report would become the basis for further studies, and especially a search for possible remedies. However, further studies had to be undertaken by a specialist institution since Kalecki's working group, after conducting this pioneering preliminary work, could at best only carry out a co-ordinating role.[10]

In Kalecki's view the report did not give a definitive answer to the question of what was at the roots of economic delinquency in the early 1960s. He himself was inclined to favour the hypothesis that economic delinquency in the socialist countries was a feature of a particular stage in their development, in which emphasis was laid primarily on rapid expansion of output. Thus, in Poland, the origins of this kind of delinquency were to be found in the period of forced industrialisation at the time of the Six Year Plan of 1950–5. In this period, he distinguished the following features contributing to economic delinquency:

(A) The basic task was the fulfilment of the production plan. Costs and quality were of secondary importance. As a result all attempts to control these aspects of enterprise activity were completely neglected. Because of the sellers' market, buyers cannot be fussy in their purchases. Misuse of materials and reducing the quality of stocks cannot be revealed by a lack of purchasers.
(B) Because of widespread shortages, it is much easier to sell articles stolen from enterprises, and at high prices too.
(C) As a result of the high share of investment in national income and the lag between the development of industry and that of agriculture, real earnings tend to fall behind the potential of the economy.[11]

The first two factors mentioned by Kalecki facilitate economic delinquency, while the third gives rise to it.

At this stage of socio-economic development, economic delinquency is fairly primitive and generally unorganised. Objective circumstances mean that neither great expense nor organisation are required. But the extent of this delinquency is enormous. This is in part due to the tolerant attitude of society at large to these abuses, which are regarded widely as a legitimate means of supplementing low earnings. In the next phase of development increasing attention is paid to cost and quality. With the gradual saturation of markets, real incomes among the population rise. Economic delinquency of the first kind ceases to proliferate. However, new forms of delinquency emerge which are more adapted to higher (but still far from perfectly effective) controls. The individual delinquent is replaced by a more highly skilled delinquent group which carries out its activities with greatly improved organisation (even at higher material cost). This greatly reduces the risk of being caught out, which in turn weakens the effectiveness of more rigorous repression.

Kalecki realised that controls were far from catching up with the activities of delinquent groups. He suspected that in at least some cases their representatives enjoyed sufficient political influence to be able to oppose controls. He wrote that

> such resistance can always be dressed up effectively as opposition to bureaucracy and saving on costly regulation. For example, for years the setting up of a quality inspectorate independent of enterprise management has been under consideration but nothing has come of it. Of course there may be other motives for opposition to such controls. Even those who are not economic delinquents have an interest in obtaining a high rate of financial accumulation through easy 'savings' of materials and labour, reducing the quality of output. In any case, the introduction of more rigourous controls is not a matter of reason alone, but a struggle against various interest groups.[12]

Despite this, Kalecki considered that it was impossible to combat economic delinquency without more stringent controls, to which adequate resources would have to be devoted. Just as for each factory its output, capacity utilisation and new investment are planned in advance, so appropriate forms of control over an enterprise's activity by agencies independent of it need also to be drawn up.

Sooner or later, any institution systematically investigating economic delinquency was bound to come up against the 'interest groups' to which Kalecki referred. There was also a climate of hostility towards establishing such an institution, arising out of the contradiction between Kalecki's tentative conclusions, which were likely to be confirmed, and the official view of the Highest Chamber of Control and the Procurator-General's office, according to which economic delinquency was declining. The studies undertaken under Kalecki's direction indicated that the actual trend was the reverse of this, and that the cause of it was the absence of proper economic controls.

In 1967, a special commission was set up to examine the whole system of economic control. No action resulted from this until 1971, when the Council of Ministers passed a resolution on the subject. It put forward 'functional' control; that is, the checking of enterprise decisions for formal conformity with regulations, but also for their effect on enterprise performance. Obviously such controls only become possible and make sense under conditions of real enterprise autonomy.

Notes

1. See M. Kalecki and L. Landau, *Szacunek dochodu społecznego w 1929r* (*An Estimate of Social Income in 1929*) (Warsaw, 1934) and M. Kalecki and L. Landau, *Dochód społeczny w 1933r i podstawy badań periodycznych nad zmianami dochodu* (*Social Income in 1933 and the Basis for Periodic Studies of Changes in Income*) (Warsaw, 1935).
2. M. Kalecki, 'Porównanie dochodów na głowę ludności pracującej w roku 1954 i 1937' ('A Comparison of Per Capita Incomes among the Working Population in 1954 and 1937'), in *Dzieła*, vol. IV, p. 369.
3. See M. Kalecki, 'Porównanie dochodów robotników i pracowników umysłowych z okresem przedwojennym' ('A Comparison of Manual and White-Collar Worker Incomes with the Pre-War Period'), in *Z zagadnień gospodarczo-społecznych Polski Ludowej* (*On the Socio-Economic Problems of Post-War Poland*) (Warsaw: 1964).
4. Ibid. The income comparisons for particular occupational groups, which were not included in this article, show that the real incomes of some highly qualified workers (for example, in the steel industry) may have even been slightly lower in 1960 than they were in 1937.
5. Ibid.
6. See Kalecki's notes, prepared for Hilary Minc, entitled 'Subsydium dla spółdzielni produkcyjnych ('A Subsidy for Producer Co-operatives') and 'Kredyty zapomogowe dla spółdzielni produkcyjnych' ('Credit Assistance for Producer Co-operatives'), among his private papers, and the archives of the Council of Ministers, AURM3/106, GM/MK/19/55.
7. See Kalecki's statements at meetings of the Agricultural and Forestry Sciences Section of the Polish Academy of Sciences on 29 May 1961 and 22 April 1963, in *Dzieła*, vol. IV, pp. 231–5.
8. See Kalecki's comment on a paper by W. Herer entitled 'Wpływ rozwoju rolnictwa na rozwój gospodarczy' ('The Influence of Agricultural Development on Economic Development'), in *Dzieła*, vol. IV, p. 358.
9. M. Kalecki, 'Próba wyjaśnienia zjawiska przestępczości gospodarczej' ('An Attempt to Explain the Causes of Economic Delinquency') *Kultura i Społeczeństwo* (1962), no. 3, pp. 73–7, and *Dzieła*, vol. IV, p. 236.
10. See the Polish Academy of Sciences' Committee for the Study of Socio-Economic Issues in Post-War Poland, Report on Activities in 1960–62, a copy of which is among Kalecki's private papers.
11. M. Kalecki, 'Próba wyjaśnienia'.
12. Ibid.

8 Kalecki's System: a Summary and Reconstruction

The elements of Kalecki's thought on socialist reproduction outlined in previous chapters are tightly interwoven. Their central point of reference is economic planning which for Kalecki was the fundamental characteristic of a socialist economy. This and his mistrust of indirect (market) instruments of central planning determined his approach to the system of economic functioning. His theory of economic growth arose out of the practice of planning. Indeed, the purpose of the theory was to improve that practice. His approach to investment efficiency analysis had similar origins. The somewhat more fragmentary work discussed in Chapter 7 also relates to various aspects of economic planning. Are these theories and ideas merely loose offsprings of his thinking about socialist planning, or are they theoretical building-blocks which make together a consistent whole? In my view they provide a consistent system of a socialist reproduction, despite some gaps and drastic simplifications in the analysis. Let us now try to reconstruct the main features of this system.

CENTRAL PLANNING

For Kalecki a socialist economy meant a centrally planned economy. After 1949 economic planning and management in Poland had been centralised to an absurd degree. As a result, in 1956, the need for any central planning at all was often questioned, whether in the hope that its functions could be performed by an appropriately devised system of economic incentives, or lest it restricted enterprise autonomy or paralysed the operations of workers' councils. Kalecki decidedly opposed such suggestions.

> No one would surely dispense with central planning altogether. However, essentially this is not a very meaningful statement, since the notion of planning can be so diluted as to embrace even

> counter-cyclical intervention in the capitalist countries. What we have in mind here is central planning . . . that embraces the volume of production, the wage fund, larger investment projects as well as control over prices and the distribution of basic materials.'[1]

Kalecki maintained this belief in the need for central planning of such broad scope in all his later work.

Together with the intellectual left in Poland during the 1930s, Kalecki was well aware that such planning requires appropriate political and institutional conditions: the nationalisation of industry, transport, the wholesale trade, the financial system and banking, foreign trade and so on. Later on, he always took into account the socio-political condition of economic planning. When consulted on economic policy by developing capitalist countries, his advice was always adapted to those conditions, indicating the institutional constraints on otherwise feasible solutions. From the 1940s onwards, he also pointed to the need to create suitable forms of social ownership and control, a system that he called democratic 'socialist planning'.

But with key sectors of industry nationalised, Kalecki did not regard inadequate progress in securing actual social control over economic processes as an insurmountable obstacle to central planning. He seems to have believed that nationalisation implied the takeover of power by the masses, and he did not question how this would operate in practice. In 1956–7, during discussion on workers self-management he was mainly concerned with the integration of workers' councils with central planning. He gave less attention to the notion of workers' self-management as a factor in developing socialist democracy and to the question of political pluralism. It was only his experiences in 1964–8 that inspired him gradually to revise his views on the importance of political conditions under which economic activity took place even in a socialist economy.

THE PURPOSE OF ECONOMIC ACTIVITY

Kalecki regarded it as axiomatic that the aim of economic activity in a socialist economy was the fullest possible satisfaction of the population's needs. Hence his emphasis on the contradiction between consumption in the short and the long run. This contradiction could be eased by careful attention to economic efficiency. But it could only be resolved by political decision. For Kalecki, full employment was partly a means of achieving this aim of fully satisfying personal needs, and partly an end in itself. He regarded the provision of a job for everyone that wanted one as an incontrovertible obligation of a socialist state, and the best way of securing for everyone a share in the realisation of that ultimate goal and an adequate standard of consumption. In this way the misery of unemployment would be removed, and differences in personal income would be restrained.

THE SYSTEM OF ECONOMIC FUNCTIONING

Kalecki did not regard the way in which the economy functions nor changes in it as a panacea for difficulties in raising the living standards of the population. He felt that these difficulties were largely the result of exogenous factors revealed in the insufficient growth of agricultural production, the slow development of primary industries and balance of payments constraints. In his view economic disproportions resulting from planning mistakes and deviations in the course of plan fulfilment were another important source of these difficulties. But the actual way in which the economy operated in the early 1950s Kalecki saw as being primarily a function of these objective constraints and structural disproportions.

The Polish social unrest of 1956 was a demonstration of workers' social pressure 'from below' which, as early as the discussion on the programme of the British Labour Party in 1942, Kalecki had recognised as a necessary condition for a democratically planned economy. It was true that in Poland this pressure was somewhat delayed and how long it could last was uncertain. But it still created an opportunity to replace the system of bureaucratic centralism with a system guaranteeing direct producers a greater share in economic decision-making and greater control over the carrying out of such decisions.

Kalecki was an active participant in the work of the Economic Council on the new economic model. Here he was against allowing industrial management to dictate the conditions for decentralisation and the extension of enterprise autonomy. He pressed for the extension of workers' self-management, as opposed to directors' discretion. But his single most important contribution to the draft of the new model was his synthesis of central planning and workers' self-management. He had no illusions that the system he proposed was free from contradictions: 'Undoubtedly,' he wrote,' there will always be a tendency in them to reduce the prerogatives of workers' councils in favour of greater centralisation, as well as a tendency for workers' councils to weaken the central plan'.[2]

Despite this, and despite the efforts required to balance the centrifugal forces in such a system, Kalecki regarded it as desirable on all accounts for two reasons. First of all, extending enterprise autonomy and creating workers' councils would contribute to raising living standards in the long run. Workers' councils which combat the bureaucratisation of the system of central planning but do not undermine that system could bring considerable benefits through releasing creative initiatives and raising productivity, especially if supported by appropriate financial rewards for the workforce. Secondly, irrespective of its economic benefits, the establishment of workers' councils should be considered an essential part of creating a system of democratic socialism'.[3]

The essential features of Kalecki's synthesis of workers' councils and central planning were a small number of compulsory aggregate performance indicators, of which the net output indicator tied the enterprise's interests to overall economic goals. The remaining plan targets either modified this transmission mechanism from the central plan to the enterprise, in order to take into account special industrial and economic circumstances, or else they limited enterprise discretion over, for example, wage increases. Workers' councils, responsible to the workforce, would help prevent abuses of working conditions, overtime payments and so on, as well as combating bureaucratisation and the return of excessively centralised forms of economic management. The opposition of workers' councils would be much more effective against this than the resistance of enterprise management which is appointed by and hence dependent upon the authorities. (Nevertheless, in retrospect, one may come to doubt whether it is at all possible for workers' councils to counteract effectively the bureaucratic tendencies of economic management without some associated democratisation of the political system.) Finally, the extension of workers' self-management up the administrative hierarchy of the economy, and the participation of their representatives in the organs of this hierarchy would better tie the interests of enterprises in with the general interest.

In current operational decisions, 'autonomous, self-managing enterprises' were to be guided by means of a suitable system of incentives. Kalecki was aware of the limitations of profit-sharing as the basis of payments to workers. He pointed out that in practice this presents various difficulties in a socialist economy which follow from a mechanical transfer of methods used in a capitalist society to a socialist one.

> In a capitalist society, no one is bothered if capitalists in different industries or in different enterprises in the same industry are 'unjustly' rewarded. Furthermore, fluctuations in the income of capitalists do not in any way have the same kind of severe adverse effects as would fluctuations in in workers' incomes, were these to depend on profit-sharing. This is for the simple reason that capitalists invest a large part of their profits. Hence even significant changes in profits may not affect the consumption of capitalists. Finally, in a capitalist society, profits are not the some synthetic indicator, but the very purpose of enterprise activity.
>
> It should be stated that the above argument is of a rather fundamental character . . . the reliance of the economy solely on enterprise profit-sharing would not necessarily guarantee rapid economic progress.[4]

Kalecki therefore proposed that the new system of incentives and directives on payments to the workforce should be linked to the growth of profits averaged out over a number of years. This was to smooth out the adverse effects on workers' earnings of fluctuations in profits while retaining the incentive towards greater efficiency. It would also resolve the problem of the initial profit differentials between individual enterprises.[5] The incentive of workforce shares in the growth of profits was supplemented by the wage fund limit. This was supposed to induce enterprises to increase net output per worker.

The effect of these incentives was further modified by the planned differentiation of profit margins. These were to be kept at the same level within a given industry in order to avoid reluctance to produce less profitable items, but set at a higher level in those industries where greater output was more important than lowering unit production costs. A system of interest charges on investment was to encourage economy of investment in increasing output and the minimisation of material costs.

As for the organisation of the agencies monitoring enterprise peformance, Kalecki sought to secure a degree of pluralism in this. Side by side with the horizontal industrial associations existing up to that time, he proposed setting up 'vertically-integrated concerns' in which enterprises would retain a high degree of autonomy. These concerns would, where possible, be self-sufficient in material supplies, and thus would include, for example, their own steel-works and machine-tool enterprises. This would simplify industrial co-ordination and input allocation. There would be a community of interests between the management of the concern and its constituent enterprises. Differentiated command and reward systems adapted to the specific circumstances of its enterprises could be applied within the concern. Kalecki also favoured a reduction in the number of levels in the hierarchy of economic administration in order to simplify it and make it more flexible.

Among the main characteristics of this model of economic functioning is that it retains direct (command-and-allocation type) central planning in relation to major development decisions and investments. At the same time it extends the autonomy of enterprises over their operational activities, while linking their production into the central plan by means of some direct and some indirect – price-type – instruments of plan construction and implementation. At the enterprise level it allows considerable scope for workers' self-management. Does this model indeed allow for the required integration of the various individual interests of the intermediate organs of economic administration, at the enterprise level and below it, with the general interests of the economy as a whole? We shall return to this question in the final section of this chapter.

A METHOD OF PLAN CONSTRUCTION

Unbalanced development not only strengthened the excessive centralism of economic management; it also drastically reduced freedom of manoeuvre in current economic policy as well as in long-term planning. At its roots lay an excessive rate of industrialisation, combined with the economic strains of the Korean War and political tensions in Europe and, on the other hand, an attempt at compulsory collectivisation in agriculture. On a theoretical level, unbalanced development was justified by the dogma of the necessity to expand production or the means of production faster than that of the means of consumption.

Once this dogma is rejected one is left with the problems of finding a guiding principle in drawing up the proportions of the five year plan, and particularly the perspective plan, whose time horizon allows for considerably greater freedom of choice of the structure of production. The obvious starting point is to determine the resources available: what the economy can dispose of during the period of time under analysis. In this Kalecki's approach to planning was more precise and realistic in its assessments, but it did not differ fundamentally from the traditional approach. The revolution that he accomplished was in the manner of plan construction, and the determination of plan targets.

Up until then, trends were extrapolated and it was believed that the faster a given sector or industry expanded, the better for it and for the economy as a whole. At the same time there were industrial and regional pressures on the central authorities aimed at obtaining the greatest possible allocations of productive resources such as investment funds, foreign exchange and wage fund allocations. Kalecki's methodological innovation was the consequence of his serious treatment of the answer to the question of what is the purpose of economic activity under socialism. If it is consumption, then it is necessary to start by defining its size and composition in the target year of the plan and the periods running up to it, as well as the relationship of consumption to the non-productive investments that form the basis of non-material personal services. Only after specifying consumption in the broad sense like this did Kalecki proceed to draw up the volume and structure of national income and non-productive investment: in effect, how much needs to be produced and invested in order to obtain the desired growth and composition of individual and collective consumption. This in turn determines the industrial structure of gross national production and non-productive investment. This sequence of plan construction was also the substance of his principle of integrating the various parts of the plan.

This change in plan methodology, discussed in Chapter 4 above, had far-reaching consequences. The requirement that plan targets for inputs and outputs be justified in terms of a socialist production target function was intended to eliminate a major cause of economic inefficiency. Kalecki's two other basic principles of long-term planning – the efficiency of planned investment, and plan realism – were also aimed at increasing economic efficiency (cf. p. 93 above). His fourth principle, that of protecting the interest of current consumption, is further evidence that Kalecki never lost sight of the fundamental purpose of economic activity under socialism.

To these four principles a fifth can be added: the principle of considering different plan variants. Its importance was frequently stressed by Kalecki. He considered it necessary to formulate alternative development variants comprising, among other elements, the size and composition of comsumption over the plan period, raw materials extraction, the application of new technologies, and the volume and structure of foreign trade. Considering different variants during the planning process would ensure that the central authorities could properly choose from among alternative development strategies. An intelligible formulation of ends and means in each variant would allow a choice to be made after a wide public discussion. This in turn would promote positive social attitudes in the course of carrying out the plan selected in this way. One can see in this the germs of an idea of the socialisation of the planning process.

PLANNING THE RATE OF ECONOMIC GROWTH

The main purpose of Kalecki's theory of growth in a socialist economy was to create the framework in which the decisions concerning the choice of economic growth rate and the distribution of national income corresponding to it, in the long-term plan, could be taken. The starting point of this theory was again the axiom that the purpose of economic activity under socialism is the raising of the living standards of the population. However, this was not enough to specify a theory of growth.

The chief way of raising future living standards is an acceleration of economic growth by increasing the share of accumulation in national income. But not every acceleration of economic growth secures higher living standards in the long run. Acceleration strategies which do not must not be followed. Moreover, even when growth acceleration does promise increased future consumption, it always reduces potential consumption in the short term. The compromise solution to this dilemma must be the subject of a political decision reconciling various interests in society, but which is itself outside the scope of the theory of growth. Therefore Kalecki accepted the valuation of short-run consumption relative to consumption in the long term as given by political factors. The central planner's trade-off between the current and the future consumption he illustrated in his Government Decision Curve.

This curve was an important concept in Kalecki's theory since it attempted to bring into the realm of central planner's decision-making various constraints on the development rates of particular sectors and industries. These constraints were due to technical and organisational factors such as limited natural resources, the length of gestation periods of investment, the slow absorbtion of technological innovation, difficulties in recruiting labour to certain occupations, the long-term nature of the process of learning-by-doing, and so on. (However, these barriers to growth were not so much an integral part of that theory as merely boundaries to the set of feasible growth acceleration strategies.)[6]

In so far as the Government Decision Curve represents the preferences of the authorities, one of its functions is to show how changes in various conditions and initial assumptions would alter the trade-off between current and future consumption. Changes in these conditions are represented by shifts in the position of the curve. When, for instance, effective constraints on the development of particular sectors or difficulties in balancing foreign trade appeared, the shift would show a reduced willingness to sacrifice current consumption, or even total opposition to such sacrifices.

The growth theory that was built up on this foundation was a purely deductive analysis. But its formal mathematical construction, presented in terms of the well-known equations defining the rate of economic growth and its corresponding share of accumulation in national income, did not ultimately determine the rate of economic development. In Kalecki's view, the ultimate determining factors were exogenous to his logical-deductive system. These were factors such as technical and organisational constraints on growth rates, and the political decisions of the planning authorities. Kalecki brought these imponderable factors out into the open from a context in which these quantitatively incommensurable elements were shrouded in routine procedures, concealed by conventional value-judgements, and confused by the vested interests of institutions and organisations. For this reason, although he regarded the theory of growth as an exact science, he emphasised that his formulation of it was by no means a comprehensive treatment of socialist economic development. Moreover, even those factors which he took into account he considered to be by their very nature debatable.

Kalecki viewed this theory of growth as the most important part of the political economy of socialism. At the same time, he was aware of its various weaknesses. In a lecture that he gave in 1964, on being awarded an honorary doctorate at Warsaw University, he gave an objective review of his own achievements and described the current state of the theory of growth in a socialist economy as follows:

> [We are] . . . only on the threshold of developing this extremely complicated discipline. We are still far from mastering even its most essential issues. Moreover, in our discussions we often fail, putting it mildly, to meet the highest standards of precision in formulation and argument. There also appears a tendency to present as axioms assertions which in fact require a proof and which, on closer examination, do not always turn out to be tenable. The further development of the theory of growth and its applications should remove precisely those differences of opinion which spring from imperfect knowledge and divert economic discussion towards those problems which the theory is intrinsically incapable of solving.[7]

INVESTMENT EFFICIENCY APPRAISAL

Like his growth theory, Kalecki's studies of the theory of investment efficiency calculations in a socialist economy arose out of the theoretical and practical needs of economic planning. In a report on the results of work started under his supervision at the Planning Commission at the beginning of 1957, he wrote:

> The fact that this work developed at precisely that time was no coincidence. In the course of carrying out the Six Year Plan, and especially up to 1954, *there was a tendency to squander expenditure on investment*, since at that time insufficient emphasis was given to securing a potentially high level of consumption in the short term. Now there emerges in its fullness the contradiction between the desire to obtain the highest possible living standards now, by having a high share of consumption in national income, and a fast growth rate of that income and consumption, for which a high level of investment is necessary . . . *One of the chief ways of easing this contradiction is by increasing the effectiveness of investment expenditure*, which enables us to achieve the same rate of economic development with a lower share of investment, and hence a higher share of consumption, in national income.[8]

Kalecki was aware that his work on the theory of investment

efficiency was more important for perspective planning and five-year plans rather than current investment. This is because when a large number of investment projects are already under way, the choice of variants and of the composition of investment is, by their very nature, limited. In his subsequent work on economic planning, Kalecki included the principle of the efficiency of planned investments among his basic principles of long-term economic planning.

The purpose of the work on the methodology of investment efficiency calculation was the achievement of an increase in national income, of a given composition and use-values, using the smallest possible investment outlays. At the same time, this calculation was supposed to secure full employment and balanced foreign trade. Equilibrium in the labour market was to be achieved by selecting the appropriate investment variants. These were not necessarily the variants that embodied the most advanced technologies and featured costly automation, especially if the same labour savings could be obtained with smaller outlays, using simpler mechanisation, more rudimentary infrastructure, and so on. The investment variants chosen were to be of such capital-intensity that the labour required in the new plants balanced the supply and demand for labour, while allowing a programme for shortening working hours to be implemented.

The choice of the most efficient target structure of consumption was closely associated with long-range planning. Kalecki himself admitted that his work on equivalent consumption bundles of varying composition, and on the choice of the variant requiring the smallest outlays, was merely a first step towards resolving this complex issue. His proposed solution presupposed a model of the economy in which the central planner, rather than directly consumers and producers, decides the equivalence of consumption bundles and their optimisation.

Kalecki's subsequent work on the theory of investment efficiency calculation was increasingly closely linked with growth theory. The notion of a production curve provided the basis of a classification of technical progress and of an analysis of economic growth acceleration by increasing the capital-intensity of production. The marginal pay-back period, used by investors in their investment efficiency calculations, was the instrument by which the central planner could induce investing enterprises to select a desired degree of mechanisation in new plant. In this way the central planner could influence the level of labour productivity. This then, combined with the rate of growth of employment, defined the rate of economic growth.[9] At the same time, this methodology allowed the choice of investment variants to be decentralised within the framework of an overall level and structure of investment. The latter were to be determined centrally in line with Kalecki's view of the permissible scope for decentralised economic decision-making.

SOCIALIST ECONOMIC RATIONALITY ASSUMPTIONS RECONSIDERED

As we have seen, the core of Kalecki's thinking on a socialist economy is central planning. As soon as this is recognised, his ideas and theories on the functioning of a socialist economy, the aggregate proportions of its development, the theory and practice of economic planning, growth theory, the methodological foundations of investment efficiency appraisal, all fall into their respective, well-defined places. This, in my opinion, warrants their treatment as a whole: as an outline of a theory of socialist reproduction. This is a theory of a centrally planned economy, with full employment, and whose sole authentic purpose is the raising of the living standards of the masses. The central planning used to achieve this is by direct administrative means, leaving indirect methods to guide merely current production decisions.

This theory is also based on an implicit assumption that the central planners can make rational decisions and have them carried out. However, the whole idea of human rationality nowadays raises many doubts. Maybe it is merely evidence of the sanguine view of the capabilities of human mind that is a heritage from Spinoza and Descartes. Even if we limit ourselves to the question of economic rationality under socialism alone, but leave aside the logic of Lange–Lerner models and concentrate instead on economic and political working arrangements in the countries of 'real socialism', this question turns out to be rather complicated.

It is possible to distinguish two fundamental aspects of socialist economic rationality. The first concerns the possibility of rational decision-making by the central economic authorities, while maintaining the internal macro-economic consistency of their decisions. There is also the extent to which these decisions can be carried out by economic agents not merely at a factory or plant level, but all along the social structure of production down to individual employees. The second aspect concerns the rationality of these economic agents, the consistency of their motivation and interests with those of the economic authorities, and even the agents' very understanding of the decisions of the authorities. Kalecki paid a great deal of attention to this second aspect, especially to the connection between favourable attitudes of the direct producers towards production, efficiency and innovation, on the one hand, and their share in economic decision-making, supervision of their work, and the related degree of social awareness on the other hand.

In the early 1940s, there was a common conviction on the left that after the War there must emerge some forms of socialist economic planning.[10] Kalecki stated then that 'as to method, democratic planning must satisfy the need of the producers (workers, technicians and managers) for some control over the activities in which they are engaged, and some opportunity for creative initiative, that is, for industrial democracy'.[11] The hopes for socialist revolution in the developed capitalist countries after the Second World War were never fulfilled. Ideas for political democratisation in Polish economic life in practice only developed in a small way as a result of the workers' protests in 1956. As we saw, Kalecki attached great weight to the anti-bureaucratic social control functions of the forms of self-management that emerged spontaneously at that time. He saw in their vertical extension an important factor integrating the interests of the workforce with the general social interest. He appreciated and greatly valued the changes in social consciousness brought about by the 'Polish October': the tangible and positive effects aroused by these initiatives in the economy and social life.

This last factor – changes in social awareness and their feedback effects on the process of socialist economic reproduction – did not just appear in the 1942 programme referred to above, or in Kalecki's pronouncements on economic management. In his work on planning and the theory of growth in a socialist economy, Kalecki insisted that ignoring the interests of current consumption adversely affects the 'socialist consciousness of the masses', but also had a feedback effect on the growth of labour productivity, the maintenance of technical and qualitative standards of production, work discipline, and so on. He devoted a great deal of attention, as we saw in Chapter 7, to these dangers.

After workers' self-management, and participation in economic decision-making, widespread understanding and support in society for central government policy, its economic decisions and those of the organs of economic administration was for Kalecki a second precondition for micro-economic rationality in the socialist economy and consistency between individual interests and the general social interest. He wrote in 1942:

> No socialist government can hope to succeed unless its efforts are seconded by a feeling of a heightened tempo of development permeating the whole of society with, at its core, a mood of determination and, above all, of *self-confidence* amongst the workers and the lower strata of society. Such a mood cannot be created artificially – it can be stimulated by propaganda, but only if a real basis for it exists . . . It is from this source that would arise the social pressure which would support and sustain a socialist government in its fight against the powerful capitalist groups and enable it to drive through its more radical planning measures. But these in turn will react upon the situation within industry, giving still more power to the workers and so further increasing the social pressure from below. The administrative measures from above and the pressure of workers from below would thus interact with a cumulative effect, sustaining the impetus of the whole planning movement and bringing about, in fact, a *continuing social revolution*.[12]

For at least three reasons, these conditions for micro-economic rationality are far from sufficient. The first concerns the harmonisation of individual and collective interests. The belief that there exists at all such a level of social awareness under which all individual and group aims and interests coincide is utopian. In any case, conflicts of interest and aims are an important motor force of economic and social development, and one should by no means attempt to eliminate them. Thus, where these do exist, a concern for the level of social awareness should be combined with care that the mechanisms for reconciling those interests are also conducive to reconciling micro-economic and macro-economic rationales.

The second concerns information flow. This does not just concern the doubts rightly raised half a century ago by F. A. von Hayek about the capacity of the central planner to obtain, process and distribute all the necessary information. Nor is it just a matter of the subjective and systematic corruption of that information by individual or group interests. Certain information is simply difficult to transmit. For example, how can one transmit intuition, experience or speculative forecasts regarding future demand, prices, technical conditions of production, and so on?

The third reason concerns what Kornai calls the 'hard budget constraint'.[13] It is of course uncertain whether the threat of bankruptcy itself is a sufficient guarantee of rationality and economic efficiency at the enterprise level. But, to put it mildly, the 'soft budget constraint' certainly is not conducive to such rationality.

Connected with these last two points is the matter of the degree to which the central and intermediate economic administration can make rational decisions and have them carried out. This is a matter with which Kalecki did not properly deal. He knew well and himself had experience of the autocratic authority on which the social unrest of 1956 had only a passing influence. But he still deeply believed, up to the late 1960s, that this authority was essentially popular and socialist, and that it at least intended to act primarily for the social good. Believing this, he implicitly attributed rationality to the decisions of the central authorities. It was true that the events of 1956 and the experience of subsequent years showed how the intentions of the authorities could be completely at variance with the effects of their decisions. The assumption that these decisions were rational could not stand up when faced with the scale of the arbitrariness that was revealed, and the mistakes in economic policy. Possibly Kalecki derived his belief that economic decisions under socialism were more likely to be more rational than in a market economy not so much from the nature of socialist authority, but more from his trust in the potential of central planning.

The potential for rational central decision-making and the carrying out of such decisions also depends on the system of political relations in society, within the centres of power, between them and the economic administration, between the authorities, social organisation, and so on. It is also conditioned by the way in which enterprises operate, which is again partly associated with political relations. It was apparent, from at least the early 1950s, that all was not well in the relationships between, on the one hand, the system of political authority and, on the other hand, the system of economic planning and functioning.

It was eventually the experiences of the 1970s that showed that without a joint analysis of the political and economic systems it is not possible to understand certain recurrent trends in the economy, (for example, quasi-cycles in investment activity), which may turn out to be incompatible with the intentions and decisions of the economic authorities. Moreover, only such an analysis can attempt to explain the behaviour of those authorities and provide the basis on which to seek out an institutional framework creating greater potential for rational decision-making.

As I have already mentioned, this kind of reflection on the capacity of the central economic authorities to make and enforce rational decisions is absent from Kalecki's work. But there is good faith in such rationality in that work. His 'centralist' inclination can be seen in this faith, which was reflected by implication in his views on the functioning and development of the socialist economy. It is precisely in this sense that his theory relates to a rather idealised socialist system.

The deep roots of Kalecki's theory in economic practice make it easy to defend against accusations of excessive abstraction and empty formalism. The famous barriers to growth, disproportions in production and so on were all phenomena which Kalecki came across and had to cope with in his everyday work. But undoubtedly this overwhelming concern for the proportions of and the barriers to economic growth and the constraints upon it tended to push into the background more general institutional structures and socio-political relations. As a result, when writing about socialism Kalecki deemed it possible to analyse the fundamental problems of reproduction in isolation from political and institutional arrangements, or at least implicitly under the assumption that they are a neutral factor. Yet this was the same Kalecki who was exceptionally realistic in seeing the links between social and political conditions and economic development under capitalism: the author of a theory of the political business cycle which over forty years ago anticipated processes in which political and economic factors interact. It can be argued in a sense that he studied monopoly capitalism as it was, and socialism as it could be. We can with hindsight see in this the source of the superiority of his theory of capitalist reproduction as compared to his theory of the functioning and development of the socialist economy.

Towards the end of his life, Kalecki departed from this one-sided approach to the economics of 'real socialism' and viewed it increasingly critically. He prepared himself for an essay on a radical reform of the socialist system. In his paper on the fundamental reform of the capitalist system, he analysed the factors which enabled capitalism to survive the unusually difficult period of the Great Crash of 1929–33 and even secure quite a long period of relative stability.[14] His essay on the radical reform of the socialist economy was to be devoted to an analysis of the social and political changes which could provide long-term stability and development for the socialist system. For he never ceased to believe that, notwithstanding, socialism could be a system of better social justice and a higher economic rationality than capitalism.

Notes

1. M. Kalecki, 'Workers' Councils and Central Planning', in *Selected Essays on Economic Planning*.
2. Ibid.
3. Ibid.
4. Ibid.
5. The realism of this solution is doubtful. On the one hand it underestimates the problems of introducing it, and subsequently of maintaining proper audit and control over it against probable systematic bias in information on actual profits. On the other hand, it would weaken the incentive effect of profits on the workforce.
6. Kalecki's approach to the problem of bottlenecks, disproportions and imbalances in an economic plan was somewhat one-sided. He saw them as being primarily due to a failure to observe the basic principles of long-term economic planning that were discussed above. However, the other side of this question lay in the actual rules of behaviour in enterprises in a centrally planned economy. The systematic analysis of these rules and a proof that inflexible prices and the 'soft financing' of enterprises must also inevitably lead to bottlenecks was only achieved towards the end of the 1970s. See J. Kornai, *The Economics of Shortage* (Amsterdam, 1980).
7. M. Kalecki, 'Why Economics is not Yet an Exact Science', *Polish Perspectives* (1964), no. 9, p. 65.
8. M. Kalecki, 'Jak łagodzić sprzeczność inwestycje-konsumpcja (o pracach nad badaniem efektywności inwestycji)' ('How to Ease the Investment-Consumption Contradiction – Studies on the Efficiency of Investment'), *Życie Warszawy*, 18 May 1957.
9. Similarly, there was a strong link between the depreciation coefficient in the formula for the rate of growth of national income, on the one hand, which was determined among others by the pace of technical progress and the supply and demand on the labour market and, on the other hand, the optimum productive life-span of fixed capital, which was used in the calculation of investment efficiency.
10. If we recall the radicalisation that took place in those circles approximately ten years earlier, when the lingering crisis of 1929–33 was often perceived as a symptom of an imminent collapse of capitalism, this conviction had in part a character of 'postponed demand'. Only later did it become increasingly clear what Kalecki had noted and warned against already during the 1929–33 period, namely that rearmament and war would provide a 'capitalist way out' of the crisis. The outbreak of

the war and its course undoubtedly boosted the popularity of economic planning ideas and projects.

11. M. Kalecki, 'The Minimum Essentials of Democratic Planning', *Labour Discussion Notes*, no. 35 (Sept. 1942). Also in *Selected Essays on Economic Planning*. It is striking that in this essay Kalecki does not mention how the 'producers' will exercise their democratic control over centrally made decisions on such matters as production, pay, investment and prices.
12. Ibid.
13. J Kornai, *The Economics of Shortage*.
14. See M. Kalecki and T. Kowalik 'Osservazioni sulla "riforma cruciale" ', *Politĭca ed Economia* (1971), no. 2–3.

Index